Introduction to Profound Prayer

Mariano Ballester, S.J.

translated from Italian
by
Bethany Lane

A Liturgical Press Book

THE LITURGICAL PRESS
Collegeville, Minnesota

Cover design by Greg Becker

This work was initially published in 1992 under the title *"INI-ZIAZIONE ALLA PREGHIERA PROFONDA,"* ISBN 88-7026-723-7, © 1987 BY P.P.F.M.C. MESSAGGERO DI S. ANTONIO–EDI-TRICE–Basilica del Santo–Via Orto Botanico, II–Padova, Italy. All rights reserved.

1	2	3	4	5	6	7	8

Library of Congress Cataloging-in-Publication Data

Ballester, Mariano, S.J.

    [Iniziazione alla preghiera profonda. English]
    Introduction to profound prayer / Mariano Ballester ; translated from Italian by Bethany Lane.
      p. cm.
    Includes bibliographical references.
    ISBN 0-8146-2430-8
    1. Prayer. I. Title.
BV210.2.B285513   1997
248.3'4–dc21

                                      97-1543
                                        CIP

Contents

CHAPTER ONE

Profound Prayer

Pray unceasingly.
(Eph 6:18)

The Parable of Animus and Anima

Paul Claudel, in one of his reflections on French poetry, presents us with the famous parable of Animus and Anima.[1] Animus and Anima are two aspects, or dimensions, of the human being. The two of them dwell in the same house, and they would be enormously happy if they understood and loved each other. However,

> things are not going so well in the house of Animus and Anima. It has been a long time now (how quickly the honeymoon passed!) since Anima has had the right to speak as freely as she wished while Animus listened to her ecstatically. Yet, is it not Anima who contributed the dowry and furthers the good fortune of the household?

Children preserve within themselves Animus and Anima in their honeymoon state; so too do poets, mystics, and artists. Both groups possess a free Anima, one full of originality, richness, and creative fantasy, together with an Animus that is simple and docile, that is all curiosity and openness, and that is delighted in its role of faithful interpreter and collaborator with Anima.

To go on with Claudel's expression of the parable:

> Animus did not put up for long with his subordinate role, and very quickly his vain, pedantic and tyrannical nature became obvious. Anima is judged ignorant and stupid, for she has not

1

gone to school, while Animus knows so many things, has read many books, has learned to speak clearly and powerfully by putting a pebble in his mouth–so that now, when he talks, he does it so well that his friends say it is impossible to speak better than he. Thus Anima no longer has the right to speak at all; Animus takes the words right out of her mouth. He always knows better how to express what she is going to say. In addition, he mixes up everything with his theories and his storehouse of learning, and states it all so confusingly that she, poor little thing, no longer understands anything.

There you have the divorce of Animus and Anima, a divorce that repeats itself nowadays in vast numbers of human beings.

Western persons are typically strongly logical, rational, critical, intellectual, stubborn–more Animus than Anima. Their culture has been formed over the centuries in an environment in which Animus exercises totalitarian influence. From the beginning of its cultural formation, the Western child learns "lessons," studies and constructs propositions, later goes on to the university "in order to know how to think," "to become intelligent." There he or she will feel overwhelmed, lost in the midst of a thousand philosophical systems and ponderings that have been piling up from Thales of ancient Miletus to our day. During this time, all that appears to the Westerner as something that eludes an exact, precise explanation, that seems surrounded in mystery or in an ascetic and religious vision, will immediately be put aside and attributed to Anima. And Anima, let us not forget, is ignorant and stupid because she has never gone to school.

Thousands of miles away one finds another version of human culture. In the Orient purely logical thought is respected but transcended, making room for states of consciousness that are beyond pure reason. Intuition, familiarity with the inexpressible and the mysterious, experience that transcends the exactly definable and tangible–these more or less constitute the basis of Oriental culture. There Anima reigns. A genuine Easterner smiles–as do the silent and enigmatic stone Buddhas–in the face of our intellectual systems and structures, our technical capacities, our exact sciences.

Naturally, exceptions exist in both East and West. Furthermore, in recent years the two worlds seem to have awakened from their isolation and to have begun looking at each other with a certain interest. However, a true harmony between Animus and Anima, one based on love, the only source that guarantees a definitive and perfect union, is still a long way from being realized.[2]

The conflictive drama of Animus and Anima is not only present in a generic divorce of two world cultures, it is also a problem for individual persons. One might say that East and West lead divorced lives in countless human beings. Each of the two dimensions tries to subdue the other; each develops itself at the expense of the other, exploiting the other and using it according to its own whim. And then the oppressed dimension, deprived of its liberty, ends by giving in, scarcely defending itself with the weapons of the weak, taking refuge, that is, in a kind of lethargy and silence, or at most collaborating with a mechanical and inexpressive docility. This is a familiar and genuine tragedy.

The authentic integration of the human being ought to take into account in equal measure both Animus and Anima, without disdaining one or the other simply because one finds oneself in a given hemisphere of the globe. For everyone possesses both dimensions. This is a universal condition that surpasses every manifestation of local culture, that goes beyond every inculturation. For this reason, when some participants in my courses in profound prayer feel antipathy toward "becoming Oriental," I invariably say to them that it is not a question of turning into an Easterner—that is, of accepting a culture, a form of life different from ours—but of becoming more completely human. Profound prayer aims, in fact, to free that half of our being that has seen itself reduced to impotence and silence during years of methodical atrophy. Little by little, that half will feel accepted and brought to its proper level in the full personality of the individual. Certainly, to achieve such an end it will be necessary to use techniques, means that are not very familiar in the West. However, they are human means that develop the inmost forces of the human being, forces or faculties that are not exclusive to the Japanese or the Oriental Indian and therefore are perfectly adaptable to our culture. In this process we hope to achieve a reharmonizing of Animus and Anima.

What Profound Prayer Is

The harmony between Animus and Anima could be approached from various standpoints, their being guests that live together in all the stages and in most situations of human life.

The present work has the aim of meeting halfway all those who feel themselves drawn to integrate their personal prayer. This mode of prayer, which certainly does not pretend to be the only valid one, we will call "profound prayer." Let us now see some particular aspects of it.

Prayer

Profound prayer tends above all to elevate us toward God. Among the many definitions that exist on prayer, perhaps the most simple and successful is "ascent to God."[3] This elevation naturally entails a continual progress, and as it develops in the individual, it needs to become more radical, more absolute, and more unitive. One can also say that the dynamism characterizing this elevation never ends, even though one has arrived, as we shall see, at well-defined goals in given moments of the ascent. In fact, the elevation is infinite in breadth, length, height, and depth, as is indeed the immeasurable mystery of God.[4]

Profundity

The ascent to God, which presupposes prayer, can start from many different levels, for not every way of prayer is equal in depth. Thus the second characteristic of this prayer is its profundity. In it one seeks to elevate oneself by beginning from the most intimate roots of one's being, that is, from the particular dimension proper to Anima—which is certainly the richest and most profound part of the human person. But as we have indicated, Anima, seeing itself continually ignored, becomes accustomed to not valuing its

riches but at hiding them with great care beneath its bashful-
ness. Let us listen further regarding the secret riches of Anima:

> One afternoon Animus suddenly entered the house. Perhaps
> after lunch he felt somewhat sleepy; the fact is that he heard
> Anima singing. She was singing alone, behind the closed
> door. It was a strange song, something he had never heard.
> He was not able to make out the notes, the words, the tonal-
> ity; it was a rare song but truly wonderful. Later he tried to
> make her repeat it, but Anima acted as if she did not under-
> stand: she became silent when he watched her.[5]

Let *us* seek to open our Anima to the ways of prayer and
to teach it to feel free, to be aware of its riches, to overcome
its timidity. In truth, profound prayer is not a very common
prayer, one to which the masses are given. It is suggested
only to those who feel and accept, in their intimate experience, that Anima is living inside them and that in a mysterious but unequivocal way is urging them to pray more deeply.

Integration

All that has been said so far could give the impression
that the author wishes to convert men and women into solitary ascetics or into mystical beings outside of the reality of
our world. But let us not forget that profound prayer intends
to integrate the person, even if in order to arrive at that integration one needs to develop, especially at the beginning,
the withered dimensions of one's being. When one's openness to God is more complete, when one's faculties, which
first find themselves in a stunted and confused state, are clar-
ified and well-orientated toward the Creator, then one will
acquire a personality that is neither tense nor frenetically active but that spontaneously radiates its interior strength. One
will thus have transformed one's life, will have found the art
of living and of sharing with others—in a harmonious, creative way—the marvelous adventure of one's encounter with
God. As we shall see, those whom we call mystics are far
from being misanthropes or incapable of an active life.

At times I have met with persons who, under the pretext
of seeking mystical experience, shut themselves up in narcis-
sistic or socially aggressive states. At the opposite end, other

persons, after their first experiences of profound prayer, have asked me diffidently and impatiently, "But what value has this in practical life?" In reality, the journey that we will map out will not look at all like either a psychic experience or a treatise on marketing. It will, however, bear in mind the body and spirit of the human being, its social and individual dimensions, contemplation and action, manifest and latent faculties. And it will seek always to sustain and integrate harmoniously all the aspects of the human personality.

Experience

The fourth fundamental characteristic of profound prayer is based on the dimension of experience. The methods used put one in contact with the world of one's experiences, helping to discover all one's riches and unsuspected secrets, including an experience that harmonizes all the various aspects of the personality. Thought is a specific human experience, but profound prayer is not only thought. Nor is it only sentiment, nor only effort of the will, nor exclusively physical tranquility. It is an integral experience in which the known and unknown faculties merge so as to perceive things in a new and unique manner. Many times this type of experience reaches the limits of human expression. However, the important thing is not to be successful at expressing it but to assimilate and live it.

Love

What has been said up to now could be summarized in this way: Profound prayer tends to free and develop in the human being all the immense capacities to love, a love that keeps on purifying and elevating itself and that in its higher levels has only a vague memory of that love—more or less limited and egoistic—that served as a point of departure.

One of the most beautiful characteristics of this love is its universality. Sensing oneself united with the Supreme Being, with the One Who Is,[6] far from limiting the individual's love, opens that person to immense cosmic dimensions and leads gradually to a love toward all creatures, animate and inanimate.

My Love, the mountains, the valleys . . . the islands . . . the rivers . . . the air . . . the night . . . the dawn . . . the silent music, the resonant solitude.[7]

This cosmic consciousness turns the ideal of profound prayer into the ideal of integration with the community, with which one feels bound on the level of universal salvation. The saying of Charles Peguy that we do not save ourselves alone is a reality that becomes a loving awareness in profound prayer. One then understands that the tiniest offense or harm done to the community, even to nature and the cosmos, is in depth a lack of love for oneself, and that the most elevated feeling of one's life consists in making oneself a channel that, with total and docile dedication, transmits the universal love of God to God's children. In such a way one understands and loves whatever is sane and authentic in political systems, in the evolution of human thought, in scientific progress. And all things enable one to realize, inasmuch as it depends on that person, one's immense ideal of universal love. This is a loving realization of the ideal proposed by the Christian prayer par excellence: Thy kingdom come.

During retreats or courses on prayer I often meet with persons who, full of good will, have struggled for years in exhausting attempts at prayer by using traditional methods. Others have simply abandoned their prayers, saying that the important thing is to serve one's neighbor. But what surprises me more is the interest that Oriental meditation techniques have aroused among Westerners in the last quarter century. The practical repercussions of these techniques, especially among the young, are truly far reaching. Today, almost everyone has heard of Yoga, of Zen, and of transcendental meditation and its ramifications in sophrology, mind control, and the like. Many contemporaries already practice these meditative disciplines. But perhaps not all have understood that the world of our Christian religious experience is perfectly compatible with the best of the techniques inspired by Eastern religions.

The Catholic bishops of the Federation of the Episcopal Conferences of Asia, coming together in their second plenary assembly November 19–25, 1978, to discuss the theme of prayer, declared:

> Asia has much to offer authentic Christian spirituality: prayer that gradually develops the human person in the unity of body, soul, and spirit; prayer of profound interiority and immanence; traditions of asceticism and renunciation; techniques of contemplation of ancient Eastern religions, like Zen and Yoga; and simplified forms of prayer such as the "namjapa," the "bhajans," and other popular expressions of faith and piety of people who with mind and heart turn themselves faithfully to God every day.[8]

Profound prayer that adapts Eastern forms of meditation is not the only way that aims at realizing the integration of body-soul-spirit. Yet today most masters of prayer have understood how urgent it is to unite the two worlds of East and West in a similar experience of prayer. To this end each of them has presented a method that obtains undisputed results.[9] A true sign of the times!

Without wishing to play the prophet, I think I catch a glimpse of a new method of prayer that is taking shape, one more valid for the people of the twenty-first century, a century already at our gates, yet one that is charged with mystery.

Notes

[1] "Reflexions et propositions sul les vers francais," *Positions et Propositions,* 1 (Gallimard, 1934).

[2] Within our century the forces for uniting the two cultures have frequently emerged. Masters of an authentic Oriental spirit such as Aurobindo and Gandhi have assimilated a Western university education, while there are numerous Western intellectuals such as K. von Durckheim who have spent part of their lives with masters of Oriental meditation. Among these attempts at synthesis, the great work of Carl Jung seems to me exceptional in its richness and depth. Still more recent is the work of Professor Haridas Chauduri, director of the California Institute of Asian Studies in San Francisco. His book *Integral Yoga* contains the best statement of his thought on the topic.

³ Cf. Ireneus Hausherr, *Priere de vie, vie de priere* (Paris: Lethielleux, 1964) 33. The other definition of prayer Hausherr gives, namely, to request from God the things that it is expedient to ask of God, supposes already, in my opinion, the first: if one really requests something from God, it means that one is already elevated in some way toward God.

⁴ Cf. Eph 3:14-19.

⁵ Claudel, "Reflexions et propositions."

⁶ Cf. Exod 3:14.

⁷ Kieran Kavanaugh and Otilio Rodriguez, trans., *Collected Works of St. John of the Cross* (Washington, D.C.: ICS Publications, Institute of Carmelite Studies, 1979) 14–15.

⁸ Session 4, 8, "Fides," Spanish ed., December 9, 1978.

⁹ Let us cite just a few examples. Notable in Spain are the courses of Nicholas Caballero, director of the Center of Interiorization and Meditation (Valencia: C. Ermita) and author of the famous book *El camino de la libertad* (Valencia: Edicep) and similar courses in prayer based on Oriental methods given by Rafael Bohigues, author of *Escuela de oracion (50 metodos para orar* (Madrid: PPC). Other masters of this sort of prayer are J. M. Dechanet, who writes originally in French; Klemens Tilmann, who writes in German, and—one of the most popular of such authors—Anthony de Mello, who writes in English but whose best known book, *Sadhana, A Way to God,* has been translated into the major languages.

CHAPTER TWO

The Desire

Observe the lilies of the field.
(Matt 6:28)

Ardent Longing

Profound prayer begins with an intense desire.

> When the flame leaps toward heaven,
> when the fire makes itself felt,
> then obstacles disappear and the darkness becomes light.

This ancient comment from the *Yoga Sutra of Patanjali* expresses symbolically all the force of the desire of the beginner who hurls himself or herself toward the ideal of purification and illumination of the mind. The force of such desire, constant fidelity to the ideal, and tenacity in the face of obstacles is called in this *sutra* by the beautiful name of "ardent aspiration."[1] It is therefore important to be clear from the beginning that if the individual does not feel a strong desire, similar to the fire that leaps toward heaven, profound prayer will not confide its secrets. Simple curiosity to be acquainted with the methods of prayer and eagerness to possess greater resources for passing the time dedicated to prayer more peacefully are very far from the genuine desire of entering into the experience of profound prayer. The story that follows will serve to orient that desire along its proper path.

The Musk Stag

An old popular legend tells of a musk stag who one day let himself be seduced by the desire of a mysterious fragrance

that lured him like a hidden call, which at times seemed
near, and at other times unattainable. From the moment the
seduction began the life of the musk stag was changed into
an anxious coming and going, in which he was unable to discover from whence came that strange and alluring scent. The
final chapter of the life of the musk stag was a tragedy: always more fascinated and beside himself with the secret attraction, he met death falling from the top of a precipice
while searching for his treasure. Only then, from his torn
bowels, appeared the broken vesicle of musk that finally re-
linquished all of its aroma in that place of death.[2]

The legend of the musk stag recurs often in diverse cultures and popular traditions, and all forms of the legend conclude with the same observation: it depicts a desire that does
not find the proper way to be realized. Indeed, the desire
aims to discover the treasure that could change one's life,
transforming it into a paradise. But according to the legend,
the treasure is either not found or is found too late.

If we look for the parallel of this legend in our daily life
we will find still other variants. First, we need to acknowledge
that this type of passionate and transcendental search is rare.
Few of our contemporaries really have the desire to embark
on a radical search, one that is vast and mysterious and that
will transform their existence into a *new life,* in a process that
uncovers unsuspected regions of the personality and eventually changes and makes luminous their barren daily reality.
Second, those who set out on such a path, and above all
those who by sheer calm and patience succeed in wearing the
badge of authentic seekers (those called saints, mystics, or
contemplatives), reveal to us ways of searching and results of
that search that have nothing in common with the obsessive
need of the musk stag. In place of a disordered and somewhat
egoistic search we find the enchantment of harmonious, constructive, and above all loving action led by the light of a wisdom that comes from within. Interior light and exterior
action, which might at the beginning have formed a duality,
little by little blend into a reality unique, personal, and completely new–that of the contemplative-active person or that
of a contemplation that has transformed action.

The fortunate people who have reached this harmonious fusion have discovered, as it were, the musk and its aroma before dying. Some are singled out and shine in history, powerfully illuminating their contemporaries. Others pass without fanfare completely unnoticed, because they belong to the category of the little ones of the reign of God, of the littlest of the little ones whom Jesus has blessed in particular and to whom he revealed his mystery. Thanks to their well-oriented desire, both the renowned and the obscure experience elevated and divinized life, giving them a dimension completely luminous. They have a holy and ineffable vision of God in all things, and all things in God.

In one of the episodes of his life, Jesus Christ, our model in all, left us an echo of this transforming and resplendent vision. Wishing to elevate his disciples beyond a myopic, calculating, and materialistic vision, he says with simplicity:

> Observe the lilies of the field. . . .
> I say to you that not even Solomon,
> with all his glory,
> was clothed as one of these.

Undoubtedly, the desire of earthly humans will find the riches of Solomon much more attractive and interesting than the humble lilies of the field. Yet Christ admired those flowers and saw that there was in them something more precious and resplendent. That "something" they also see who, looking at the earth (this our earth, resistant, according to some, to every effort to see it as manifesting the divine goodness) burst forth into a song of benevolence and love, because in the earth they see none other than the love of the Creator. Rather, they see the Creator in all creatures:

> The Beloved is the mountains
> the valleys lonely and rich in shadow,
> the remote islands
> the murmuring waters
> the whistling of loving gentle breezes.
>
> He is as the calm night
> very near to the rising dawn,
> silent music,

resonant solitude.
He is the supper that refreshes and fills with love. . . .[3]

Praised be you, my Lord, with all your creatures,
especially Sir Brother Sun
who is day, and you illuminate us by him.

And he is beautiful and radiant with great splendor:
of you, most High, he brings meaning.

Praised be you, my Lord, for Sister Moon and the Stars:
in heaven you have formed them clear and precious and
beautiful.

Praised be you, my Lord, for Brother Wind
and for air and cloud and calm and all weather. . . .

Praised be you, my Lord, for Sister Water,
who is most useful and humble and precious and pure.[4]

It is not enough to have a burning desire. It is necessary
to know how to elevate it and orient it toward its most precise goal. This is not always easy, for in the process a great
number of doubts and prejudices and a strange and latent
aggressiveness assail us with a force and an obstinacy equal
to the same force of desire with which we began.

Is It Really Possible?

Poetically symbolized in the legend of the musk stag, the
problem is as old as humanity itself and appears in practi-
cally all the great religious movements. Unfortunately, the
easiest and most frequent way of confronting it is that of
skeptically asking oneself, "But is this life transformed in
contemplation, this interior light, etc., is it really possible, re-
alizable in practice by the man or woman in the street?"

Anyone who asks a similar question is already giving
themselves, implicitly, a negative response; and it is like sign-
ing the death sentence to the least effort necessary to begin
to walk the contemplative path. Unfortunately, our mentality has the primitive and stubborn tendency to believe ab-
solutely impossible or unrealizable all that one does not
personally know. And the skepticism will be all the greater
as the system of thought is more narrow. "Few are they who

take to heart the task of examining carefully and seriously that about which they express their judgments. Nothing limits the vision more than one's *system* of thought, because it excludes other aspects of reality, which then do not enter the enchanted castle of the fixed pattern that one has in one's head."[5]

In the end we are obstinate positivists who, even when we consider the lilies of the field, are not willing to see in them more than form, measure, and specific weight. We think that to know them truly is to touch them and analyze them with acids, checking their molecular structures and chemical reactions! Naturally, therefore, we appreciate much more the sumptuous and magnificent clothes of King Solomon, more pleasing to the senses and more useful than the poor cellulose colored lilies of the field.

> However, I say to you
> that not even Solomon,
> with all his glory,
> was clothed as one of these.

Here exists the great enigma of the lilies of the field. But from the moment that, in spite of every obstacle, we continue to consider ourselves followers of Christ, we really ought to find the solution to the problem of the lilies, which is a problem raised by Jesus himself. Sooner or later, however, most of us prefer to take refuge in a sphere all our own, that sphere in which, as we have seen, we Westerners move like fish in water–the world of conceptuality, where Animus reigns.

Persons of Western culture who possess an ordinary intelligence have minds similar to Pandora's box: with much pleasure and facility we offer theoretical solutions for every contingency and every problem. It is necessary then that we now examine, with the relative risks of brevity, the principal conceptual solutions that, up to now, men and women have found for responding to the enigma of the lilies of the field.

First Solution: Theoretical Faith

A first solution, one that strongly entices our mind, is to affirm that it is a question of faith. To be contemplatives in activity is to believe that God is in all things. Our lack of faith, therefore, is the only culprit if, in the bustle of daily life, we are neglectful of contemplation, the one thing that could make us be continuously mindful of the presence of God.

The world of faith, then, is another box of Pandora for explaining the unexplainable. (Naturally, we are not here speaking of true faith, which is something vital, but a theoretical faith.) For, having recourse to this solution of a greater or lesser faith, we are, without realizing it, intellectualizing both faith and the problem. To see God in things in this case would be in some way to *think* of a God in things. That would turn out to be in the best of circumstances a devout exercise of Christian reflection that has nothing to do with the world of contemplation. Our basic point here is that the faith of the true contemplative-active person is experience, while that of the devoted thinker is faith-thought and is much more limited than the authentic vital experience of Christian faith. As to the capacity of thinking of God continuously in daily actions, I doubt that anyone could endure such a thing for a long time without breaking, not indeed the belly as the musk stag did but one's own head—and without obtaining even a drop of perfume in the process. Of course, before reaching such an extreme situation we excuse ourselves by saying that we have still not arrived at such high levels of faith as to be a contemplative-active.

Second Solution: The Two Sisters

The second theoretical solution goes back for centuries, to Martha and Mary, the two sisters of Lazarus, in whom tradition has respectively symbolized action and contemplation. In general, the tradition does not present the sisters as being in great agreement. We say, with relief, that one cannot be both at the same time. They embody distinct vocations. God calls some persons to the state of the purest contemplation and destines others to the undertaking of Christian action. It is a question, therefore, of something that does not depend on us but on the gifts that the Creator liberally distributes. Thus the most contemplation one will be able to get, especially among religious of active life, will be to dedicate some quality time during the day to prayer. But (persons of active life are apt to think) God mainly wishes that we dedicate ourselves—with the same fervor and interest that we have for prayer—to our daily work, to a work already sanctified by our preceding prayer.

We could expand here upon the fratricidal polemic that has filled so many pages of Christianity over the centuries. Whoever desires to enrich themselves with reflections on the debate can have useful recourse to the exegetical comments of tradition on the gospel passage of Lazarus and the two sisters. But what truly interests us at this moment, in the intricate labyrinth of reasons for and against the way of one or the other sister, is to discover the leading thread of all, which is, still, the theorizing intellect. To consider the approaches of the two sisters brought together in only one reality appears incomprehensible to reason, because reason is always perceived as embarrassed in the face of the union of the one and the many. We have an allergic reaction to seeing God within ordinary activity. It almost arouses in us the fear of being transformed into rare, unnatural beings, as would happen to the Israelite people when somebody merely suspected that God was near to them (thinking they would die).[6] We think immediately of eccentric behavior, as if we were schizophrenics acting with two personalities. Hence the many intellectual digressions in the history of the exegesis on the two sisters—all aiming finally at reconciling them with each other.

Third Solution: To Pray Is to Live

A third solution, much more modern and simple, is that of quietly affirming that *for me prayer is life*. A most beautiful expression, certainly, almost a panacea, a universal remedy. But here too we have an evasion of the real and exacting exercise of prayer, in the hope that the life we lead can indeed be described as Christian. I surely do not intend to deny that living is to pray, if this signifies discovering a new life in the light of an interior wisdom such as that permitted the contemplatives to see God in all things. But I am still doubtful about whoever has superficially changed this quest into the formula "for me, to pray is to live," because such a path is quite distant from resembling the life of authentic active-contemplatives. Later we will speak concretely of the authenticity of the testimonies of these true active-contemplatives. For now it will be enough to understand that once again we find ourselves in theorizing, in simply verbalizing the problem.

All these games of words and ideas have a common denominator: they put aside the mysterious and ineffable experience of life. None of the solutions indicated above—or others, more or less similar, that we could list—really see anything more than the color, form, and specific weight of the lilies of the field. All of them come down to ways of thinking about the lilies. But Christ speaks clearly to his followers:

> Observe the lilies of the field. . . .
> I say to you that not even Solomon,
> with all his glory,
> was clothed as one of these.

And so, very simply, Christ destroys our complicated games and places us before the tremendous mystery of the poor lilies that are worth more than all the glory of Solomon.

Christ wishes to make us understand that whoever feels the sincere desire of solving the enigma of the lilies, of Sister Water, and of "silent music" does not need to use pure reason. It is necessary to find a new road, of which the first step, following the terminology of the Oriental mystics, consists in going out of the cave of conceptualization.[7] Once outside that cave, it is necessary to walk toward the inside of another chamber (one's heart or soul) and avoid the externalization that is our habitual tendency. One needs to close one door in order to be able to open another. The task is to grow in an understanding of that inner universe, as it was understood by St. Augustine, who, guided by his immense desire and illuminated by interior wisdom, could exclaim:

> Stimulated to re-enter into myself, under your guidance, I entered into the intimacy of my own depths, and I was able to do it because you became my help (cf. Ps 29:11). I entered and saw with the eye of my spirit, such as it was, an unalterable

light over my own interior gaze and over my intelligence. It was not any earthly and visible light that shines before the gaze of every man. Rather, I would be saying too little if I decided that it was only a light stronger than the common one or even so intense as to penetrate everything. It was another light, very diverse from all the lights of the created world. It was not from above my intelligence as the oil that floats on the water, nor as the sky that extends over the earth, but a superior light. It was the light that created me. And if I found myself under it, it was because I had been created by it. Whoever recognizes the truth, recognizes this light.[8]

It is a question of a totally different method than we are used to. One that is not outside but inside us, and in which we are not to lead but to be led. It is a question above all of love: of that ardent loving desire that recognizes and resolves all enigmas,[9] that converts into reality that which by human wisdom would only be absurdity: *"My Beloved,* the mountains."[10] And beginning to love, we begin to see:

You are my God, I long for you day and night. As soon as I recognized you, you lifted me up on high so that I saw how much there was to see and which by myself I would never have been in a position to see. You dazzled the weakness of my vision, shining powerfully inside of me. I trembled with love and terror. I found myself far away, as though in a strange land, where it seemed I heard your voice from on high, that said: "I am the food of the strong, rise up and you will possess me. You will not transform me into you, as food in the body, but you will be transformed in me."[11]

Notes

[1] Cf. *Yoga Sutra of Patanjali,* 2, 1, 32–43. This *sutra,* or series of little spiritual verses, is one of the classic books of the Indian scriptures, entirely dedicated to the theme of meditation-contemplation. It is the fundamental text of Raja Yoga, or Yoga of mental elevation.

[2] Cf. H. Caffarel, *Presence a Dieu, du Feu Nouveau* (Paris) 286.

[3] Spiritual Canticle in *Collected Works of St. John of the Cross,* trans. Kieran Kavanaugh and Otilio Rodriguez (Washington, D.C.: ICS Publications, Institute of Carmelite Studies, 1979) 14–5.

[4] Raphael Brown, trans., *The Little Flowers of St. Francis* (Image Books, 1958) 317.

⁵ R. Assagioli, *Psicosintesi* (Rome: Mediterranee) 24.

⁶ Cf., e.g., Judg 6:22; 13:22.

⁷ "Conceptualization is a deadly obstacle for the yogis of Zen, more dangerous than a poisonous serpent or ferocious beasts. . . . Brilliant people and intellectuals always live in the cave of conceptualization; never will they in their actions be able to go out of it. As many more months and years pass, so much more do they shut themselves up in it. Without noticing it, the mind and conceptuality are gradually made one thing only. And even if someone wished to go out of it, he or she understands that for them it is impossible. One can, at times, escape before wild beasts or poisonous serpents . . . but there is no way to escape a conceptual mentality." Chang, ancient Zen master, cited by William Johnston: *Silent Music* (London: Collins, 1974) 57.

⁸ *Confessions of St. Augustine,* trans. F. J. Sheed (New York: Sheed & Ward, 1943) 145.

⁹ Cf. 1 Cor 13:1–13.

¹⁰ *Spiritual Canticle,* 14–15.

¹¹ Augustine, *Confessions.*

CHAPTER THREE

Desires

The light shines in the darkness.
(John 1:5)

The Sirens

Ardent aspiration, the luminous force of the desire for God that catches fire in the human heart, is not alone. With it live together a thousand other desires, some evident, others not. With these other desires the pilgrim will gradually need to come to blows when, free from the quibbles of Animus, he or she gets ready seriously to follow the guest of their greatest aspiration. Along the way toward the light, desires are as sirens, enchanting mermaids: they confuse us and attach themselves to lesser goals. Disorienting the searchers, they cause them to lose their way, just as happened to the musk stag.

The infinite variety of the desires of humankind can extend from the more primitive instincts of eating, sex, and self-preservation to love of family, to aesthetic feelings and responses before natural beauty, and even to the very desire for perfection. Open any newspaper or magazine, look at the news and the advertising pages, and you will find yourself face to face with the world of passions and desires most common to twentieth-century human beings. You will see depictions running from hate to the vendettas that foment wars to the propaganda of a consumer society that promises happiness thanks to cosmetics, soft drinks, new detergents, and automobiles offering the least fuel consumption and the greatest comfort. Read the titles of movies and television shows and you will have a summary of the four or five sources that today excite and direct the major part of the life of the average person: titles of violence, of immorality, of science fiction and fantasy, of the pursuit of sheer light and sound experiences, and on and on. What is one to do in the face of this endless sea of desires?

Undesirable Desires

At this point it is necessary to offer a little explanation. Not all desires are evil; on the contrary, by nature we cannot live without desires. Our vital dynamism would cease at once if we did not feel desire. The important thing for the pilgrim of ardent aspiration will be to uncover evil and undesirable desires in order to get rid of them. But of course it will be essential for the spiritual traveler to satisfy basic human necessities in order to continue the journey. He or she will need to take into account certain elements of being that can help to reinforce and develop the desire for contemplative light: a healthy curiosity to know, a poetic sense, and above all, love in its various manifestations—these can be as so many signals that indicate the road. Later on, all this will be sublimated and become stabilized in profound prayer, as those who pray move toward the sole center of their aspiration.

The saints of every age have known and combatted undesirable longings. St. Ignatius of Loyola called them "disordered affections," and his famous book *Spiritual Exercises* has precisely the scope of liberating men and women from undesirable and destructive affections and rendering them free from attachments in order to give themselves totally to the will of God.

The Most Subtle Traps

The most dangerous desires that our wayfarer meets do not always originate from the outside. When in the hours of silent, prayerful search a person experiences at the same time the force of the irresistible aspiration toward God and a clear and undeniable obstacle, he or she then seems to hear the gospel text: "And suddenly, leaving their nets, they followed him" (Matt 4:20). This bare sentence of Matthew is sometimes given as an example of promptness and diligence in following the call of God. But it was only a beginning response, a necessary beginning but too rapid and simplified for definitively discovering the perfume of the musk. The sons of Zebedee would become embattled in nets much more subtle and dangerous than those they had abandoned that day on the bank of the lake; they would be entangled in the nets of their own interior obstacles.

In his autobiography the great Bengalese mystic Paramahansa Yogananda recounts that in his adolescence he met a holy man who said to him regarding such tremendous and treacherous interior obstacles,

> The struggles in the fields of battle are reduced to insignificance compared to the struggles that man needs to face, right from the beginning, against his interior enemies. These are not just common enemies that can defeat one with a determined display of force! Omnipresent and implacable persecutors of man, even in dreams, fortified by deceptive and unhealthy weapons, these soldiers of ignorance and concupiscence do everything possible to destroy us. Foolish is the man who buries his ideals and surrenders to his common destiny.[1]

These subtle nets can be manifested in the form of fears in the face of confusion and the unknown. The desire not to be disturbed and not to give up certain comforts in one's inner, spiritual house is at times stronger than the very physical and immediate desire of material well being. Professor J. B. Lotz, expert in the knowledge of the interior way, says:

> In this process of internalization, we abandon the settled house we have constructed. Each one constructs a house where he/she lives, from which every so often, it is necessary to go out in order to start walking. Certainly, this house protects us from whoever might harm us, but at the same time, if we find ourselves too tied to it, it impedes the influence of God. In the process of internalization, we go beyond the house where until now we have lived and set out on the way. It is true that we then expose ourselves more easily to temptations, but we expose ourselves also, and above all, to the

grace of God. I wish to say by this, that true meditation does not exist without risks and perils.[2]

The travelers, therefore, will sense within themselves all those "alarms," those irrational fears that urge them to stop, turn around, and return to being like "everyone else." For after all, they are at the point of hurling themselves toward the unknown. They are like the newborn who is leaving the secure place of the maternal womb, or like parachutists on the point of letting themselves fall into space for the first time. But in spite of a reluctance in the face of what is unknown—above all if this unknown reality is an irrational, unpleasant, and unyielding experience—we must force ourselves to conquer the reluctance and accept the experience.

Fear of Being an Island

Among the most subtle nets that ensnare one from inside is the inclination to be normal, a person of the times and not a rare specimen. The fear of ridicule, of sticking out from the usual, of not being accepted, is one of the most disguised manifestations of the ordinary human being's instinct for self-preservation and self-affirmation. Used to moving inside well-defined limits where normality is the standard (with exact limits set by the society of consumers), he or she can obviously think that all the fire of burning aspiration is like playing music that is too lofty. "No man is an island," will say our contemporaries, making their own John Donne's immortal sentence, so effectively used in our time by Thomas Merton. And it is true that the possibility of being converted into a spiritual island is repugnant to our human nature and even more to Christian charity. But the anticontemplative use of the expression manifests an illusion caused by our aversions. Whoever wishes to examine close at hand the life and personality of those who have been transformed by the light of ardent aspiration will verify that they are anything but islands. The contemplative, in cloister and outside, is an active contemplative, that is, an open-hearted person, understanding and attentive to the needs of others, integrated in the human community, and often very popular and sociable.

Some years ago the psychiatrist Kenneth Wapnik, in a comparative study of mysticism and schizophrenia, compared the autobiographical writings of St. Teresa of Avila with the diary of a "mystic" schizophrenic.[3] The fundamental difference the psychiatrist found was that the diary of the schizophrenic revealed all the signs of that person being unequivocally an island, unadapted to and disassociated from ordinary life, while St. Teresa manifested her luminous depth integrated in action and daily occupations. The light certainly was making her different: a light that instead of detaching her from reality was transforming her and empowering her to contemplative action. It is clear to whoever knows the active temperament of the saint that her humor, her capacity to attune herself to persons extremely diverse in culture and character, her creative and organizing gift, completely prevents one from classifying her among the remote psychological islands in the human ocean.

One arrives at the same conclusion examining closely the incredible activity and influence of St. Bernard in the religious and political thought of his time; the running of the people in the small town of Ars in search of its humble curate; the curious gallery of characters of czarist Russia with the thousand adventures that populate the life of the Russian pilgrim.

The light of the ardent desire of the soul is not cold but hot and radiant. It illuminates men and women as being brothers and sisters,[4] independent of their willingness to accept this fact or not.

Jerusalem

In the face of obstacles aroused by desires, the searcher needs to raise the gaze more than once and fasten it on Jerusalem.

When the pilgrims of Israel were preparing for the pilgrimage to the Holy City, they knew very well that a tiring journey was awaiting them. If the caravan came from the north, they suffered disagreeable descents near Jericho, the suffocating heat of the region near the Dead Sea, and the desolation of the desert of Judea. But once beyond the Valley of the Patriarchs and arriving at Khan Lubban, the sight that presented itself to their eyes changed their fatigue into a song of alleluia: there on high, as a crown upon the top of the mountains, shone Jerusalem, with the Herodian Temple covered with gold leaf sparkling in the sky. The vision was so luminous and exalting that the pilgrims, forgetting the discomfort of the journey, burst into the song of the famous *Psalms of the Ascensions:* "I raise my eyes toward the mountains. . . ."[5]

To raise one's eyes toward the mountains, to somehow contemplate the luminous vision of the end of the journey, is always an effective tonic against the doubts and resistances of our nature. For the Jews, the vision of Jerusalem, without negating the difficulties and risks of their pilgrimage, confirmed the authenticity and validity of the entire journey. Similarly, for us it will be helpful to fix our gaze every now and then on whoever has already carried the spiritual journey through to the end. It will encourage us to observe how, among so many persons—different in character, profession, and social status—there exists something unchangeable and mysteriously precious, some quality that blossoms and decidedly distinguishes them from the average person.

If the seeker is the humble country curate whom his companions in the seminary hold to be a nonentity, a fiasco of intelligence, the light of interior desire will elevate and exalt him so much above his contemporaries that he will draw toward his poor little country church the intellectuals and most famous preachers of France.[6]

If the searcher is a Manichean philosopher[7] and one of the greatest thinkers in history, the light of interior desire will make him stand out to such a point that his works will be read by both theologians and simple people, by young and old, transcending time and gaining immortality.

The divine desire will be able to be enkindled in the heart of the poor artisan of czarist Russia:[8] the simplicity of language with which he recounts his experience will have an unmistakable echo of geniality. His only written work, simple and humble as he, will go around the world and be translated into all the principal languages, and even today be esteemed as a true jewel of the literary and spiritual heritage of humanity.

Even a "wandering and restless" woman can be a creature who embarks on the search for the light and finds it.[9] Her personality will then acquire unsuspected and gigantic dimensions. It will influence millions of people of every class, who will faithfully follow in her footsteps. In spite of their intricate and disorganized style, her writings will be exhaustively studied and commented on by theologians and other persons of the spirit of every class and race.

Perhaps the wayfarer in search of the light desires to remain completely unknown by his brothers and hides behind the veil of anonymity. The inevitable will then occur: just one of his books, a very small one, will be enough to immortalize him precisely because of the same anonymity that he intended to maintain. People will call him the author of *The Cloud of Unknowing.*[10]

Finally, if the luminous point catches fire in the heart of an insignificant apprentice tailor, who also is a house painter and carpenter[11] and who lets himself be led until the luminous point is converted into a "living flame of love," then that fire will illuminate forever wise men and theologians of the Church from East to West.

The "vision of Jerusalem on the mountains" can be a comfort and stimulus for whoever faces the difficulties and aspirations of the way, whether that one is a curate, a philosopher, a farmer, a restless woman, an anonymous man, or an artisan apprentice. All have offered a helping hand and have left us a message: Raise your eyes toward the mountains! Look toward Jerusalem!

The fire of ardent aspiration will, little by little, yet certainly, transform the life of the pilgrims, who will draw near to God, who is the light itself.[12]

This, then, is the principal work of whoever possesses this interior light alongside the darkness of other, egoistical desires: to free oneself from every attachment contrary to the light so that the light may illuminate an ever clearer and simpler path. In a word, the task is to prepare the ways of the Lord.

Notes

[1] Paramahansa Yogananda, *Autobiography of a Yogi.*

[2] J. B. Lotz, lecture given in Rome at the Ignatian Center of Spirituality, November 15, 1974.

[3] Cf. Kenneth Wapnik, "Mysticism and Schizophrenia," *Journal of Transpersonal Psychology,* vol. 1, no. 2 (1969).

[4] Cf. John 1:11.

[5] Ps 121:1.

[6] Kathleen O'Meara, *The Cure of Ars* (Notre Dame, Ind.: Ave Maria Press, 1942).

[7] Cf. Augustine, *Confessions,* 4.

[8] Cf. *Tales of a Russian Pilgrim.*

[9] Kieran Kavanaugh and Otillo Rodriguez, trans., *Life of Saint Teresa of Avilal,* vol. 1 of the *Collected Works of St. Teresa of Avila* (Washington, D.C.: ICS Publications, Institute of Carmelite Studies, 1976).

[10] The best known book of this anonymous fourteenth century English mystic is *The Cloud of Unknowing.* See Ira Progoff, trans. (New York: Laurel Book, Dell Publishing Co., 1983).

[11] As an adolescent St. John of the Cross was a humble worker whose earnings relieved the poverty of his family, which his widowed mother was trying her best to keep going.

[12] Cf. John 1:9.

CHAPTER FOUR

Physical Purification

> *If your body is all luminous,*
> *without having any part in*
> *darkness, all will be luminous,*
> *as when the lamp lights you*
> *with its gleam.*
>
> (Luke 11:36)

Some of the unruly desires that hinder the development of ardent aspiration originate from one's own body. Some people will be astonished to learn that their elevation toward God is grossly curbed by material desires. In reality, this is so frequent and familiar that we hardly notice it.

Together with the normal and healthy needs that the instinct of self-preservation and protection of life impels us to satisfy, a thousand other artificial needs infiltrate us, needs that are in fact induced by large, including multinational, commercial firms—in short, by all those who manipulate a consumer society.

One could live equally well (indeed, freer and happier) without the infinite attractions of style, cooking, makeup, and other refinements for oneself. With ever more dangerous consequences people get used to breathing artificial products, perfumes, tobaccos, and contaminated air: they get used to letting themselves be driven by multiple and continually changing tastes even in the choice of magazines and entertainment. It is not strange, therefore, that the well being of a man or woman finds itself a prisoner and slave of his or her own material desires. We have already said that not all desires, including those that seek a legitimate physical comfort, are to be suppressed.

However, a little sincere realism will be enough for us to recognize that our level of physical-corporal life often remains hypnotized and beguiled by a thousand useless things.

Purification of physical desires, then, is necessary; and to attain it there exist various methods and exercises suggested by Eastern Yoga and by the modern sciences of Western anthropology.

First we will concern ourselves with methods that facilitate physical equilibrium during profound prayer. But we will extend these methods to daily life in order to establish general aptitudes toward a bodily purification—all this to reach that condition needed for the balance and purification of the body: *the state of physical relaxation.*

Relaxation in Specific Positions

Muscular relaxation is the necessary antechamber of profound prayer. Many do not know the great Christian tradition in this regard. Masters of prayer like St. Teresa of Avila, St. Ignatius, St. Francis de Sales, and especially the Fathers of the Eastern Church have always underlined the necessity for those who pray deeply of putting the body in serene harmony with the spirit so that the mind is not disturbed by physical tensions.[1]

Physical relaxation and balance will also be an immense antidote against the unhealthy demands of the body, beguiled by useless desires.

We will first of all consider some relaxing positions. Indian Yoga knows innumerable positions, or *asanas,* for bringing the body to a state of equilibrium and comfort that can remove any physical preoccupation from the consciousness. Some Indian theories speak of 8,400,000 possible positions of the body! Modern Yoga methods greatly reduce the number of such positions. We will limit ourselves to indicating only some of these, the ones that are easiest and most interesting for bodily relaxation and that favor the inclination toward meditation.

The Corpse

Among the easiest and most accessible exercises to us Westerners is the position of the corpse, called in Hatha

Yoga *shavasana*. This exercise is done lying down on one's back on a hard bed or on a blanket on the floor. The arms are extended along the body and somewhat away from it; the palms may be turned upward or downward but are always relaxed and open. Some masters recommend that the head remains a little elevated by a pillow.

In this position one begins by breathing deeply two or three times, mentally relaxing the individual muscles, from the head to the toe. In the beginning one will notice that some muscle or other remains tense, that it does not relax easily. It will be enough, then, to mentally gaze at it without making judgments, such as "I am tense for this or that reason," or even "I command this muscle to relax." Such judgments would only be an intellectual or emotional complication that would disturb this relaxation exercise. Rather, one just mentally attends to the tense muscle, as though the mind were a beam of light. After a few minutes one will notice that the muscle is yielding, putting itself in harmony with the rest of the body.

This position is highly recommended in Yoga to facilitate the circulation of the blood, but above all for producing total relaxation. Some Yogis judge it without hesitation to be the best position for meditation. We Westerners feel some aversion to this way of praying because we approach it, of course, as the position of sleeping. Yet St. Ignatius in his *Spiritual Exercises* recommends this position as one of the possible ones for praying.[2] One day during a retreat for religious of different nationalities, a young Vietnamese nun came to me with great wonder: "This position has been a true discovery for me. I can concentrate easily and pray as I have never done in my life!" All her life she had prayed on her knees, following the formation she had received in the West. And so, we often give these gifts back to our Eastern friends! Easterners tend by nature and tradition to the maximum integration of the person, which facilitates much more the action of the Spirit of God, who prays within us.

The Western Lotus

K. Tilmann, in one of his books on meditation,[3] offers an easy and interesting variant of the famous *padmasana,* or supreme lotus position of Eastern meditation:

Fig. 1

> One sits without resting the spine, almost on the edge of the chair, so that the relaxed and protruding knees remain lower than the torso. The legs cross at the top of the ankles, and the tips of the toes rest on the floor (see fig. 1). The hands are placed one on top of the other, formed like two cups, the left above the right, in front of the abdomen, touching it, while the wrists rest on the upper thighs and the thumbs are raised up and touch at the tips.[4]

With this detailed description, Tilmann intends to ensure the greatest physical equilibrium. It is not necessary, however, to attend rigorously to all the details, for one must not go against the tranquil flexibility and physical freedom sought by profound prayer. There are persons, for example, who because of physical limitations are not able to hold themselves erect or are made nervous if the torso is not supported by the back of the chair. In any case, the Eastern masters unanimously insist on the necessity of remaining very erect in the position of meditation. I advise beginners to experience for themselves the difference between praying erect (whether supported or not) and praying while curved or bent. The capacity to perceive things at higher and more delicate levels is much greater in the erect position, but it is only experience that will demonstrate this.

Once settled into the position, one begins to direct awareness toward the sensation or feeling in the right hand. It is not a matter of *thinking* of the hand but of sensing it. The consciousness needs to focus on the *sensations*. Remaining some moments on each sensation and starting from the right hand, one proceeds slowly thus: sensing the forearm, the upper arm and right shoulder; the left shoulder, upper arm, forearm, and left hand. Then one repeats the procedure in reverse a little more quickly. One will thus arrive at creating a *circle of sensations* that rotates around the center of gravity of the body, situated in the lower abdomen. Very quickly that will put the person in a state of physical relaxation and calm. With time that calm will transmit itself to all the body, and the person will find himself or herself in a perfect equi-

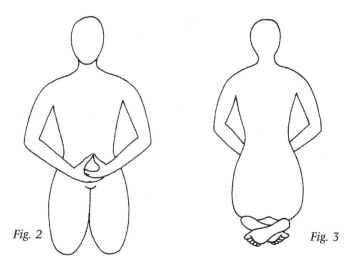

Fig. 2   *Fig. 3*

librium, ready to venture beyond the threshold of profound prayer.[5]

The Suwari

The *suwari* is a position much used among the Japanese but is known also in Yoga by the name of *vajrasana,* or position of the diamond.

One kneels down and crosses the feet lightly. A little at a time, one sits down on the heels. The back needs to remain as erect as possible for the same reasons given in the preceding exercise. The hands can be placed as in figure 1 or even placed gently on the knees (see figs. 2 and 3).

This position produces a sensation of calm, equilibrium, and serenity. Besides, it strengthens the muscles, joints, and nerves of the legs.

In beginning the exercise one may encounter a certain difficulty, experiencing pain in the joints of the legs and feet. To avoid this, one can put a blanket (rolled up or doubled) under the feet. The exercise may also be done by sitting down on a very low stool instead of on one's feet, thus evading the pain and obtaining almost the same effects as in the classical *suwari* (see fig. 4).

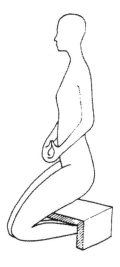

Fig. 4

Whatever variation of the *suwari* is used, one obtains the same muscular relaxation that is achieved from the practice of the Western lotus.

Another simple relaxation exercise consists in counting the breaths up to ten, taking care to breathe only through the nose. After completing the series, one then begins again and continues to repeat the count until attaining a calm and interior serenity.

Other Positions

The way of purification and spiritual equilibrium is obtained first of all by experience and not by theory. Therefore, I warmly advise all who desire to progress not to draw back from such exercises, at least not before having practiced them. The positions advised by Hatha Yoga for meditation and psychological balance such as the perfect position, the half lotus, and the lotus (see figs. 5, 6, 7, and 8) are also suitable to Westerners—especially those who are young or who apply themselves with lively interest and perseverance. Any book of Hatha Yoga gives all the necessary details for practicing these *asanas*. Without doubt, the position of the lotus (see fig. 8) is the most suitable for concentration and deep meditation. For many Oriental schools it is the best posture

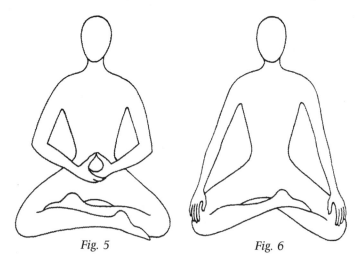

Fig. 5   Fig. 6

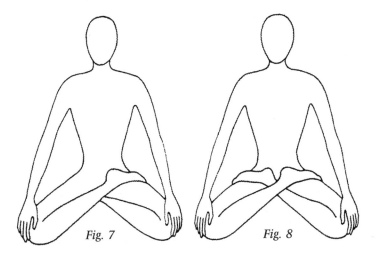

Fig. 7   Fig. 8

or position in Yoga. My professor of Hatha Yoga, Dr. J. Clement Vaz, said, "If you practice the lotus position during meditation, you will go so far as to forget you have a body." And the Upanishads say, "The position of the lotus [*padmasana*] is that which cures all sicknesses and poisonings."[6]

None of the positions must ever be used with tension or suffering. At the most, one practices the exercise until feeling a mild or moderate discomfort, and then one stops. With constancy in performing the exercise, the discomfort diminishes little by little until one day it disappears completely, leaving the individual in the ideal condition for deep prayer.

Time and fidelity to practice are necessary. In my own case, ten years were necessary before I succeeded in practicing my meditation position without any aching at all.

Relaxing Daily Movements

Purification of physical-corporal desires is not attained solely through the practice of such specific positions during prayer or meditation. The serenity and interior calm attained by these exercises vanish as soon as the person is put in contact with his or her work ambience and ordinary daily life. It will be enough to listen to the news on the radio or the constant appeals of advertising for the world of emotions and desires to be set into motion and for tensions to be aroused. It is necessary, therefore, to extend our physical control, with something of the patience and constancy we have in the exercises, to the various parts of our whole day. We can even learn to treasure the difficulties that present themselves in the course of our long meditative training, never forgetting to feed our ardent aspiration and turning our gaze frequently toward Jerusalem.

In general we can say that a slow and tranquil rhythm in physical movements (one that is not synonymous with laziness) favors contemplative harmony. That essential calm, so beneficial to both physical and psychological health, certainly does not come easily amidst the rhythm imposed by modern life.

If we could see, for one moment, the enormous quantity of physical energy consumed daily in completely useless movements and muscular tensions, we would be amazed! Go out into the street and observe people: nervous hands and gestures, hard-set faces, feet stamping the ground waiting for the bus. Torrents of energy are wasted each day in useless chatter, in making so many gestures that are done simply to be doing something, or by saying something because others do not support being together in silence or because one worries about not being sociable. Frequent headaches, nervous exhaustion, stomach ulcers, and so many other woes—so common in our day—stem more often than one would believe from such uncontrolled and continuous waste of energy.

If, on the other hand, you know someone who inspires depth in you and communicates such depth to you, that person certainly does not belong to the agitated and tense spirits that populate our society. An ancient Tibetan proverb describes the riches of a calm rhythm:

> When the hen rests, she gives much fruit,
> When the regal peacock remains immobile
>   it shows a splendid tail.
> When the horse runs slowly,
>   then one notices its grace.
> The calm of a holy man
>   is a sign that he is a Wise man.[7]

To facilitate the essential habit of a continuous muscular relaxation and calm during work and ordinary activity, there is a very simple exercise: several times a day *observe fleetingly and with tranquility* your own physical gestures. (It has already been said that the general orientation of the exercises tends to a reduction of our movements. The exercise in observing now to be described will flow nicely from the formal meditative postures. This observational exercise is not difficult in itself. Its only difficulty might consist in reminding ourselves to do it during the day, so that one might eventually acquire the habit of an *ongoing* muscular relaxation).

So, interrupt for a few moments whatever you have been doing and take account. Observe your muscles through a rapid muscular perusal of the body. Note where the muscles are tense, where some contraction has formed, even a little one. In the beginning the more exaggerated tensions will be noticed: for example, lifting the shoulders without reason, contracting the forehead and eyes while reading, stiffening the back and stomach. A little attention alone will be sufficient, an interior glance toward the tensed part and this member becomes happy and relaxed again. At most one gives a gentle interior command to the tense muscles; they will obey and relax immediately. Pay attention, however, not to carry out the exercise with a sense of hostility toward your own body, but guide and coax it as one teaches a child how to walk. Little by little, you will develop a sort of second nature about this muscular inventory; and you will instinctively discover the slightest tension, until you attain a general rhythm of calm and continuous control of your physical energies.

The good results of this exercise will come as soon as one begins to practice it: the usual moments of tiredness will disappear and work will proceed with more precision and efficacy. Desires and useless tensions that were interfering with tasks will cease and give way to a healthy and harmonious use of one's energies.

All that has been said about the control of physical/muscular energy applies similarly to verbal energy and the control of that mass of words uselessly spoken every day. Recall the admonitions of the apostle James on the dangers of an unguarded tongue.[8]

To achieve physical purification a certain moderation and balance in food is also desirable. I am not speaking of fasts or fads but of knowing how to be moderate. The book of Sirach contains wise advice in this matter.[9] And on the subject of food we find guidance in the New Testament–directions for an even higher spirituality. Let us remember, for example, how Christ recommends to his followers not to preoccupy themselves with eating but to give preference to the things of the kingdom.[10] St. Paul later writes to the Christians of Rome that the kingdom of heaven is not a matter of food and drink but of peace and profound joy in the Holy Spirit.[11]

Notes

[1] Cf. M. Ballester, *Experiencias de oracion profunda* (Madrid: PPC) 22–6.

[2] Ignatius of Loyola, *Spiritual Exercises and Selected Works*, ed. George E. Ganss (New York: Paulist Press, 1991) 76.

[3] Ed. Queriniana, 1974.

[4] Op. cit., p. 56.

[5] Ballester, *Experiencias*, ch. 2, 47ff.

[6] *Trishikhi Brahmana Upanishad*, 39.

[7] A. C. de Koros, *Tibetan Studies*, 0. 19 (Calcutta, 1912) text 20.

[8] Cf. Jas 3:1-18.

[9] Cf. Sir 31:14-25; 37:27-31; Prov 23:20f.

[10] Cf. Matt 6:25, 33.

[11] Cf. Rom 14:17.

CHAPTER FIVE

Emotional Purification

Blessed are the pure of heart
for they shall see God.
(Matt 5:8)

The Bazaar of the Emotions

If you have ever had the opportunity to visit the neighborhood market of some large European or Asian city like the Chor Bazaar of Bombay or Porta Portese in Rome or the Rastro of Madrid, you will have seen curious little scenes. I know well the Porta Portese market in Rome. In the morning of any Sunday of the year, beyond the arch of the famous gate, you feel yourself suddenly assailed by the pounding and thundering uproar coming from right and left, from interminable narrow streets crowded with buyers and sellers. Near the flower stall are objects made of crystal and representing fish and exotic birds; nearby are stalls filled with old used books, remade clothes, rusted utensils, pictures, and metallic objects of no artistic value whatever. And then the voices, the sounds, the most diverse clamors. An old man who sells bagpipes and continues to try them out, a loudspeaker at full volume that thunders with a strident melody of the latest style and repeats with cheerful offhandedness, "Stolen things!" A large, fat vendor assails you and asks, "Where do you keep your money?" Another calls you aside mysteriously to tell you of the sale of the century: precious stones, forbidden amusements, Oriental clothes, exotic objects.

Amidst this sea of things, even more curious and interesting than the scene itself is the one who observes it, the one who is wandering about in that bedlam with hands in pockets (partly to prevent someone from increasing the "stolen goods") and with eyes, ears, nose, and all the senses immersed in that multicolored and hypnotizing confusion.

Such a spectacle seems to me the perfect image of the world of the emotions and sentiments of modern humanity, continually bombarded by solicitations and desires offered by a consumer society. To stop, to close your eyes, to reflect, to leave that hypnosis and check your own emotions, is not at all easy. For one needs to struggle against the spell of the bazaar of the emotions.

For years I have listened to people of every social class who in their sincere search for the Lord have had to deal with the inevitable spell of embarrassments, irresistible attractions, uncontrollable fears, jealousies, passions, timidities, rancors, dislikes.

To mold human affection is a true work of art. The holy truth that the Indian anchorite said to Alexander the Great, "It is easier to conquer kingdoms than to dominate oneself," can be applied especially to the affective and emotional world of human beings. Excellent people, full of good intentions to form themselves and others, remain blocked for years, advancing little or not at all in the way toward God because they are not yet reconciled and purified in their emotions. It has to be said clearly right at the beginning: a life agitated by emotions cannot capture the beauty of the silent and tranquil light that delights the contemplative, of that light that appears at the end of one's ardent aspiration. Those who continue to be immoderate and restless cannot receive the superior food of the spirit. "For as long as there are among you envy and discord, are you not of the flesh and do not conduct yourselves as ordinary men?"[1] In a way parallel, then, to physical-muscular purification, there is need to acquire emotional purification.

Undesirable Emotions

An understandable difficulty arises at this point: some may think that a utopia is being proposed to them! And they may ask: "How is it possible to live without emotions? Can one even imagine in a modern progressive society that one could live insensitively to what surrounds us, closing our eyes before the problems of the world? Are not the emotions, in fact, a richness?"

Though at times the thought is not adverted to in a clear way, one almost fears *not* being able to live in a world without emotional problems. The mechanism of these cases, well known in psychiatry, can be reduced to this: "What will I do if I do not feel any stress?" Or more pertinently: "If my spiritual life does not have any complications, how is it possible that anyone–priest, psychologist, friend–take an interest in me?"

In speaking of emotional purification I do not mean to refer to an *absence of emotions*. It is, rather, a question of making a selection, of maintaining desirable emotions (which will always need to be more sublimated and transformed) and controlling the undesirable. An emotion is undesirable when it provokes in the nervous system alterations that are detrimental to physical and psychic health or engenders spiritual agitations that upset interior peace and serenity.

Emotional purification may appear to be an egoism that allows an excessive preoccupation with one's own interiority, but in reality whoever works for personal emotional improvement automatically works for the emotional improvement of the environment in which he or she lives. It does not take a lot of reflection to understand that parents who do not control their own emotions transmit part of their imbalance to the children, raising fears, timidities, aggressiveness in them that jeopardize their development and emotional maturity. The same occurs in the field of social relationships, in friendships, in work. The great truth proclaimed by St. Paul is verified in daily life: "Many are the members, but one only is the body. The eye cannot say to the hand: 'I have no need of you,' nor the head to the feet: 'I have no need of you.' Now you are the body of Christ. Every one of you is a member of it."[2]

It is impossible to make a complete and detailed exposition of the exercises advised by different schools of Yoga for emotional purification.[3] And to these exercises one would need to add others offered by modern psychology. For the moment two simple techniques used by Yoga seem sufficient here. The first refers to the more superficial elimination of detrimental emotional energies. The second requires a full and complete participation of all one's faculties, including the subconscious.

Exercise 1: Chakrasana

There are moments in which a person has the need to vent definite nervous tensions. When the husband returns home from work and shouts at his wife and children; when the adolescent bursts out unexplainably in a word of anger; when one, on certain days, appears unbearable–these are common cases in which human nature unloads emotional tensions. At times one has need of unburdening oneself with force, and suddenly. If one does not, one represses an undesirable emotion that, in time, provokes disturbances worse than the simple "letting off steam." However, it is important that the venting does not cause damage to others but occurs in the most favorable and controlled way possible.

In general, one can say that whatever physical movement can produce tiredness–running, swimming, playing ball, working in the garden–can become a simple opportunity for scattering emotional tension. If we do not have a garden in which to work, or a place to play sports, we can at least close ourselves in a room and do the following exercise, which in classical Yoga is called *chakrasana*, or position of the wheel.

Standing with the legs a little separated and the arms extended along the body, one begins by bringing the hands together and interlocking the fingers of the hands and raising the arms while breathing deeply, until the hands are above the head and as far behind as possible, thus bending the back to the maximum. At this point one holds the breath for five seconds; then while exhaling one bends forward and lowers the arms–with the hands always intertwined–until the hands are on the ground. Then, while inhaling one raises the arms to the overhead position again and repeats the exercise three or four times. Carrying out this exercise rapidly and with energy, one imitates the movement of the woodcutter using the ax. Besides stimulating glandular activity and the gastrointestinal organs, this exercise discharges nervous tension. Its easy execution makes it feasible for everyone.

Exercise 2: Affirmation

The use of brief affirmations, repeated several times as auto-suggestions, is a typical technique of mantra Yoga for controlling destructive desires and helping us to free ourselves from them. When one is struggling with an undesirable emotion, one can, following certain conditions, control it by means of a brief mantra. Let us imagine, for example, that a woman suffers from jealousy or from a possessive love. Her autosuggestion could be this: "I am perfectly happy, even if I do not see so and so." If an individual is worried by a responsibility or by a situation that he or she does not know how to deal with, the person can say: "In this responsibility or situation I listen to God: I am happy, normal, congenial; I am a child of God," *calm, at peace.* Such mantras, if repeated often enough, become extraordinary means of emotional purification.

The indispensable conditions for the efficacy of the mantra are the following:

1. Relaxation. The individual needs to be free from the interference of physical sensations—excessive heat or cold, bothersome sounds, the possibility of sudden interruptions. As noted in the preceding chapter, it is necessary to put oneself in a relaxing situation.

2. The best time is just before going to sleep. St. Ignatius also suggested this time for simple affirmative prayer to whoever was doing the spiritual exercises.[4] The mantra is also advisable in the morning right after waking up, remaining in bed during the affirmation.

3. The affirmation must be brief, not complicated or negative (never "I will not be afraid" but rather "I am courageous"), and it must be concerned with the present, not the future.

4. The repetition of the mantra is done in the following way: one begins pronouncing the affirmation clearly and out loud, then lowering the voice until one is just whispering. The affirmation penetrates thus into the consciousness (indeed, it is capable also of strongly influencing the subconscious).[5]

5. It is desirable to carry out the mantra also during the day. There are masters who even advise writing it in various places where one lives—on the worktable, on the mirror, on the cover of the notebook.

Even if this exercise is not, strictly speaking, a prayer but a technique to control undesirable emotions, it can be made somewhat prayerful. Some people obtain greater efficacy choosing as their mantra a biblical phrase indicating a virtue or the presence of God, for example, "blessed are the meek," or "the Lord is my rock."

Exercises for a General Purification of Emotional Life

The two preceding exercises serve to control a given emotion. One ought not move directly to controlling a second emotion until one has succeeded in eliminating the damage of the first. Nevertheless, we can train our general attitudes in order to control in their complexity *all the damaging emotions*. I emphasize this because there are of course emotions and sentiments that are completely positive and that greatly help us to realize the mission God has entrusted to us. It is a matter, therefore, of not permitting negative emotions and sentiments to appropriate our personality and damage it. To this end one can apply to the emotions the same general exercise of relaxation advised for the physical positions described in the preceding chapter.

To learn to observe (look at, take account of) our emotional tensions *as though we were an outside spectator* will help the relaxation and purification of this important level of the person. The object is not to *think* about those emotions, reflecting on them from above or judging the suitability or danger of them, but to isolate the emotion through a brief, sudden impression. What is needed is a simple ascertainment of an experience, which one observes quietly until it dissolves as salt in water. Once the emotional tension disappears, one ceases the exercise.

Watching the emotion from the outside, what once was hiding in obscurity now comes in to the daylight of observation. This simple observation dilutes the emotion, freeing the individual from its poison.

Before practicing this exercise, people usually think it will prove to be strange and difficult to impassively observe their feelings of strong antipathy, of rancor, of egoism. As soon as they begin to experience it, however, the hesitancy disappears. Psychologists know well that here lies an important law of our psychic life.

A relevant aspect for controlling emotions is offered by people who live around us. We have said that there are persons who radiate interior peace and calm; others are restless and agitated. It seems these latter have need of absorbing other people's vital energies in order to feed and maintain theirs. In our encounter with such people it is necessary to make it understood, calmly and tranquilly, that we are not the least interested in becoming like them or contributing to their becoming more agitated and restless.[6] Whoever has succeeded in purifying their emotional state will irradiate happiness and optimism. Instead of coming to blows with others or fixating on the negative and bitter aspect of things, this person will understand how to go beyond bitterness and sufferings by lavishing generously all the fragrance and peace that Christ proclaimed in the Beatitudes. But the best fruit of emotional purification is the progressive increase of a great love that was first a prisoner in the darkness—a love luminous and universal, free from petty attachments and egoistic interests, signs of which are clearly listed in the famous hymn to love in the first letter of St. Paul to the Corinthians.[7]

Notes

[1] 1 Cor 3:3.

[2] 1 Cor 12:20-27.

[3] One finds ample exercises for the control of emotions in the excellent work of C.E.S. Ral, *Yama*, vols. 1 and 2 (Rome: Mediterranee).

[4] Ignatius of Loyola, *Spiritual Exercises and Selected Works*, ed. George Ganss (New York: Paulist Press, 1991) 73.

⁵ The technique of the mantra, applied to the core of oneself, can be found in the precious book of Paramahansa Yogananda, *Scientific Healing Affirmation* (California: Self-Realization Fellowship, 1974).

⁶ Other exercises for pacifying the emotions are given in M. Ballester, *Experiencias de oracion profunda* (Madrid: PPC) 27–34.

⁷ Cf. 1 Cor 13:4-7.

CHAPTER SIX

Mental Purification

Do not conduct yourselves
anymore as the pagans, in
the vanity of their mind,
blinded in their thoughts,
outsiders to the life of God.
(Eph 4:17-18)

The Mobility of the Mind

The mental level is the most difficult to purify. The mind penetrates every activity of the other levels, physical and emotional, and identifies itself with them. To purify the human mind signifies, therefore, to purify the whole person.

The principal characteristic that one observes in an unpurified mind is its mobility. In the *Bhagavad-Gita,* one of the most well-known and venerated sacred books in India, Arjuna, a man who is searching for his own liberation, speaks to God in these terms concerning the difficulties met in quieting the mind: "The mind is restless, turbulent, obstinate, and powerful. To dominate it, it seems to me, is more difficult than to control the wind."[1]

The mobility of the mind has been compared by Eastern writers to the endless and acrobatic leaps of the monkey on the branches of trees. It has also been compared to the swimming of fish, as the mind wanders here and there in an ocean of ideas.[2]

Western contemplatives too are used to confronting this inveterate enemy of calm and interior serenity. St. Teresa speaks, as many do, of the difficulties met by those on the point of silencing their own mind, difficulties that she herself experienced in her efforts to pray. The noisy mind (Animus, who wants to interfere in the song of Anima)[3] is compared by the saint of Avila to a restless traveler who has no wish to return home to rest but who, on the contrary, "is looking for other places to stay."[4] At other times, she compares the crowded mind to a pile of large pieces of wood that suffocates the weak spark of the presence of God scarcely lit in the depths of one's being.[5] She compares it also to a dove that flies restlessly here and there in search of food, without entering into its dovecote,[6] and to a colony of bees that work outside the hive.[7] The restless mind is a searcher of reasons, controversial[8] and shrill;[9] it is an unhappy husband who harasses his spouse.[10] In a word, it is a fool, or even a madman.[11]

All these images give us the idea of how much effort is involved in the pacification of the mental level. If you wish to confirm experimentally that your mind is similar to the restless traveler, simply close your eyes and try to reduce to immobility the flow of your thoughts. The wandering mind will put into action all its craftiness in order to flee and avoid the invitation to repose and calm. How, then, do we obtain repose for this vagabond?

The Practice

In the *Bhagavad-Gita,* this is the reply of God to the difficulties of Arjuna about the mobility of his mind: "It is certainly very difficult to dominate the restless mind. It is possible, however, thanks to constant practice and to detachment."[12]

Once again we are led by this reply to a fundamental point of Oriental wisdom. It is not enough to complain about the mobility of the mind. It is not sufficient for the spiritual director to recommend that the disciple "fight against distractions" and drive them away. Such complaints and exhortations, if they are worth anything, will be but the preamble to the true *exercise* of mental purification. Whoever desires truly to reach the ideal of one's ardent aspiration will need to be an apprentice, to begin to *make use* of certain means, or human faculties. If a woodcutter cuts wood regularly for some months, his muscles will certainly acquire new strength and vigor. For the learning of a language, the constancy of practicing ten minutes a day is more efficacious than doing three hours only on an occasional day. The same principle is valid for the exercises to produce mental calm, and they must be used by the person who truly desires to pacify and quiet the mind. One must, then, be persuaded that no one else can do for us the concrete, hard work demanded for a purification of our own mind.

Before we describe the exercises in detail, we emphasize that the meaning of the training must be kept well in mind. An erroneous and detrimental way of pacifying our mental state is to want to confront the restless mind with brute force. The contribution of the will is certainly necessary. But its assignment is not to subdue the wandering mind; rather, its task is to transform it into a *vigilant* mind. The task of the will is to keep the traveler in a state of vigilance.

Exercise 1: Pratyahara

The *pratyahara*, or withdrawal of the senses, is a very ancient exercise practiced especially in Raja Yoga. It consists in habituating the mind to a dispassionate and disinterested exercise of self-observation.

After retiring to one's quiet place of meditation and choosing the physical position that most helps to balance the faculties, the meditator tries to relax completely and observe his or her mental processes.

The snake charmer lets the reptile wriggle, and it goes out freely from the hamper; the charmer has only to watch. Similarly, while carrying out the *pratyahara*, the observer takes into account that the mind can adopt tortuous and complicated movements and states. It is important to remain seated and in the position already chosen, with the chest erect, and observe in a detached manner, without becoming frightened or surprised, how much passes through the mind.

I caution the reader that in practicing this exercise one can run into some dangers. When one practices the *pratyahara* deeply relaxed, phenomena independent of one's willing can break loose, since the will does not become at all involved in this. One only observes. And the subconscious can reawaken and manifest its not-always-agreeable contents. An experience such as this was had by a psychologist who was passively watching the invasion of these unexpected contents. He described it thereafter in this way:

> That day I felt very relaxed and I got up right away; all around a great silence prevailed, and everything was favorable for concentration. I lit the incense and seated myself on the cushion to meditate. At the beginning many pleasant sensations possessed me: I felt full of calm and sweet happiness. Suddenly temptation assailed me. First was a thought of rebellion, more or less confused, which afterwards was made ever clearer: why was I not always able to feel as quiet as I did at that moment? Was it because I had needed to suffer so much in the past and I will also have to suffer so much in the future? It is difficult to describe that temptation, but it was more or less this. Then suddenly a great fear took hold of me and I did not know any more what to do, this amidst an infinity of thoughts and turbulent temptations that even now, in referring to them, frighten me.

The experience of the psychologist was not exactly a temptation, because neither an incentive to evil nor a distortion of values was clearly present. We can, however, affirm that within the experience there was the spirit of evil, whose intent is to create restlessness and confusion. But it is always possible to surmount with the help of divine grace, faith, and prayer whatever temptations may be lurking in such experiences. Experiences of this type are very rare, however, in psychologically normal people, who are free to interrupt the *pratyahara* when they wish. If as one continues to practice the *pratyahara* such experiences were to present themselves habitually, it would be better to interrupt the practice for a little time and consult a psychologist or other specialist.

Exercise 2: Nispanda Bhava

For purifying the mind before sessions of classical Yoga, Dr. J. Clement Vaz recommends to us the practice of the *nispanda bhava,* or simple awareness of sounds. It consists in relaxing quietly and opening our awareness to all the possible sounds around us. The awareness needs to be completely passive, that is, it must not fix or concentrate on a determined sound. As I find myself in an ocean of sounds, I need to let myself be carried along by the sonorous waves, both the nearer and the farther and more imperceptible that strike my auditory sense. Thought should not interfere at all. It is possible that at the beginning I spontaneously think, "there, that is the sound of a car," or "now it is of a door that is opening." But the ideal is to silence even this intellectual specification about the origins of the sound by simply receiving and listening to it. After ten minutes the *nispanda bhava* already produces an effect of great peace and interior purity. It has the same advantages as the *pratyahara,* and besides, it is simple to practice and is not at all risky.

Exercise 3: Cleanliness in Mental Attitude

This exercise is not practiced separately, that is, within a scheduled period of profound prayer. Rather, it has the function of creating an attitude, and one practices it, therefore, when and for as long as one wishes.

In my courses on meditation I advise this simple exercise for purification at the mental level: *observe the thoughts that go on during an ordinary day,* in the way stated above. Persons who practice this exercise for the first time are surprised by the quantity of thoughts that pass through the mind, even when there is no need to think of anything particular.

During the span of the day, it is necessary to learn to make impromptu visits to our mind. Watching your thoughts, you will become aware if in your work you keep your mind quietly on what you are doing, or if, on the contrary, your mind is occupied in useless thoughts, which take energies that divide and distract you from the occupation of the moment. The energy that one loses in these thoughts and inward talk is precious, and its loss causes fatigue. The disposition to mental vigilance will make thoughts that are useless and extraneous to your occupations disappear and will keep your mind relaxed and tranquil, occupied only in that which you are doing.

The Clear Mind

Among the salutary effects attained by mental control is a greater clarity and purity in the thought process. The one who does not waste mental energies will concentrate quickly and easily, will focus with greater precision, and, notwithstanding this intense concentration, will not feel weakness or weariness.

A clear mind is not lazy or egotistical. Its field of interest will not be centered exclusively on matters of its own advantage. It does not think, "Only that which pleases me interests me; that which doesn't please me does not interest me!" The clear mind has completely open horizons and does not look at things from the point of view of personal advantage but in the light of their natural meaning and depth. Valuing things as they are will in time reveal the true reflection of the God who clothes the lilies of the field with divine splendors.

The person of clear mind possesses a constructive and positive philosophy, can see clearly the limited dimension of creatures, but understands it as a limitation that has its ordained place in the general cosmic effect of the divine economy of Providence.

Because of this the person of clear mind does not fall into the trap of negative philosophy, of bitter criticisms, of corrosive and vicious thoughts. Such a person is a free being who generously controls his or her enormous mental energy, using it to edify the reign of God and not to confound or divide self or others.

St. Paul exhorts the Christians of Ephesus not to live as the pagans do "in the vanity of their mind, blinded in their thoughts," but "to renew yourselves in the spirit of your mind," putting on the new man, created according to God in justice and in true holiness.[13]

An Ascesis for the Modern Person

At times one feels like saying that today we have rejected and forgotten the ascetic element so much in force in the Christian training of the past. I would say that an ascesis that responds to the necessities of the modern person needs to orientate one toward a way of reeducation and of continual cleansing of one's faculties. In such an ascesis persons of today can avail themselves of all the technical richness offered by the progress of human science. Most often the greatest difficulty encountered in the distracted modern personality is the fact that those without control and not trained in the three dimensions that we have pointed out do not take into account the seriousness of their state, and they blame external life for the confusion that is inside them. One acts like the musk deer in the mountains that looks desperately for a treasure where it will never find it.

Today we certainly do not use whips or hairshirts for mortifying the body. But the poisonous distractions and enticements that were able to debase the person of yesterday have the same destructive power for the contemporary person. To limit oneself to merely wiping out what has gone out of style—that is, the severe physical asceticisms of the past—is to worsen the situation. An ascesis adequate for the perils of today (which it would be ingenuous to ignore) is therefore essential. For this reason I have spoken in clear-cut terms of the lack of control of the modern person and of the waste of physical, emotional, and mental energies. If we cast a comprehensive view on that lack of control we will have an idea of the frightening disorder and disintegration in which many of our contemporaries live. Let us imagine a person with the television continually turned on, the radio at full volume, with the cooling and heating systems, the electric kitchen appliances, and the lights often functioning day and night without necessity. If, in the face of that squandering, such a person would say to us: "What do you want me to do! I cannot do otherwise. This is my way of life!" What would we think of that person?

By offering practical exercises I have sought to support the elemental requirement of the triple cleansing of the faculties by one who wishes to reach out toward the light to which ardent aspiration leads. It is a first step, without which the impurities of the three dimensions of the human being will prevent a free path toward the light that shines in the darkness. All the roads walked upon by the contemplatives over the centuries passed through these three dimensions. We believe that twentieth-century persons are no different from their predecessors, from the active contemplatives of the past. Perhaps in the face of this prospect some, like the squanderer in the example already described, will think that the cleansing required is too much and that their life is structured otherwise. But this reply is one of so many mirages, the fruit of one's own darkness. It is not a matter of obliging our faculties to do extraordinary things but simply of training them so that they are what they ought to be and act according to the marvelous design their Creator has for them.

So as not to feel overburdened by the methods shown above, anyone can freely choose the exercises most adaptable to purifying the part of themselves that has need of more peace and luminosity.

God has not made us for confusion, for tension and darkness, but for light. As one begins to reeducate the faculties, one will need to have the loving patience of the father intent on reeducating the son who has lived a long period of his life without any control. The reeducation is possible because it consists simply in straightening our faculties and bringing them onto their natural path. Without this sound formation divine help will always find a wild terrain in us, one that may be entirely too harsh for cultivation.

Notes

[1] *Bhagavad-Gita,* 4, 34.

[2] Cf. Ernest Wood, *Concentration: An Approach to Meditation* (Madras, India: Adyar, 1966) ch. 4.

[3] See page 5.

[4] *Way of Perfection,* 31:8.

[5] *Life,* 15:6.

[6] Op. cit., 14:3.

[7] Op. cit., 15:6.

[8] Ibid.

[9] *Life,* 15:7.

[10] *Way of Perfection,* 31:8.

[11] Ibid.

[12] *Bhagavad-Gita,* 6:35.

[13] Eph 4:17-24.

CHAPTER SEVEN

When Life Is Purified

O Lord, our God
How great is your name
over all the earth.
(Ps 8:2)

In the preceding chapters we have seen the necessity of a triple purification as prior to and an irreplaceable condition in the life of profound prayer. This purification of the three principal levels of the personality–physical, emotional, and mental–creates characteristic effects that we can sum up in the expression "depth of life." To be deep is not yet to be contemplative or, as the Orientals would say, illuminated. But this deep and radical purification of the being is always essential in order to be able to arrive there where ardent aspiration tends.

A Sequence of Situations

One can make a private examination of one's own life in order to know the degree of profundity and, consequently, the degree of purification of our faculties by practicing the following exercise:

Seated, or in an ordinary position of repose, try to pacify yourself with some simple techniques of relaxation. Once quiet, direct your attention to the events of your life that occurred most recently: for example, from your getting up today until the moment in which you are reading these lines. From this period of time, choose a sequence of situations of about ten minutes duration. Then, minute by minute and second by second, try *to live these situations once more*, aiding yourself especially with your imaginative memory.

It is important not to think merely about what you have done. That would be easy and would not serve this exercise. The more complete task is *to live once more*, with total exactness and meticulousness, that given time span. It is necessary to enter into contact, as intensively as possible, with the same sensations you have already lived, the same feelings, the same great and small reactions, apprehensions, and so forth, in order to recontact everything, just as it happened.

It is possible that in doing the exercise some people encounter "blank areas." It can happen, that is, that one is not able to continue the exercise because, at a given moment of the sequence, one has no more awareness of what happened. Let us suppose, for example, that I am reliving what happened to me from the moment of breakfast until going out into the street. I see myself and can tell that I am finishing breakfast: I fold the napkin, say good-bye to those present, leave the dining room, pass the vestibule, and place my hand on the doorknob to open it. I relive the metallic sensation of the knob in my hands and after that . . . nothing more. Then I deduce logically that I must have entered the elevator and gone out into the street, because I well remember having greeted the porter when I left. But such reasoning, though valid in itself, is not really part of the exercise. As we have said, one must not deduce anything, neither thinking nor reflecting, but only recalling the actual experience. It happens that it is simply impossible for me to recall *how* I spent my ride in the elevator.

What happened? Simply, my consciousness decided that it was not interested in carefully living the time passed in the elevator, a moment so habitual that it did not draw my attention at all. I lived that time, therefore, superficially. The following diagram will illustrate everything better.

Let us suppose that this circle represents our life. If our basic attitudes remain by preference in zone S (surface), then we will be superficial, that is, our life will be a continuous succession of insipid events that are scarcely remembered. If, however, we ordinarily live in zone C (center), our actions and all our life will be profoundly rich.

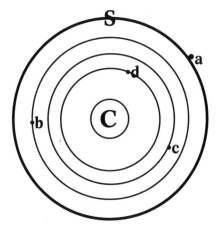

We can place the "blank area" of the example reported above at point *a,* that is, in the most superficial zone, where one has lived without feeling anything in depth. Nor has anything been assimilated at that point. There has not been any experience but just empty time, lived uselessly. Part of a dying life.

Points *b, c,* and *d* indicate a progressive interiorizing of our vital capacities. Whoever succeeds in living on some occasions in zone C, in one's center, is then living totally. That person's perception is indelible, clear, offering a true and profound enrichment. In the measure in which our vital capacities are approaching the center, we will be profound and we will possess an inexorable vital richness. If, on the contrary, we approach S, we will be lacking depth, notwithstanding the uproar or the great hustle and bustle of activity. In zone C the water remains motionless and crystalline because it is deep. In zone S the water is agitated and cloudy. Life experienced in S is diluted rapidly, leaving nary a trace, while that in C remains forever, as a hidden treasure in the depths of the sea.

Some Testimonies of Vital Depth

When the personality has acquired this triple vital purification, it undergoes many experiences of depth. There are moments in life—regardless of one's age or what the occasion is—in which people find themselves suddenly concentrated and profoundly in harmony with that which they are living. To confirm this fact, I present four testimonies. Later we will see how they arose out of a growing profundity.

Testimony A: The Yellow Envelope

At this very moment, I ask myself if I have truly enjoyed the beauty of a yellow envelope that rests on my table and attracts my glance as I write these lines. I look at the envelope, I close my eyes and think of its color. Then I open my eyes and better observe the beauty of the yellow color that I have in my mind. I feel a new enjoyment, a vital intensity as an immediate result of this little but fruitful action, and I take into account with gratitude the pleasing company of this modest yellow object.[1]

Testimony B: The Rain

We spent some weeks in the south of Spain, in the hottest period of the year. Every morning, very early, my son appeared at the balcony of our hotel to see what kind of a day we would have. Every day was the same: sun, always sun. But one morning I heard a shout of joy: "Hurrah! It's raining!" What a spectacle. Water fell from the upper streets and the roofs! What joy to breathe clear air and the smell of wet earth! That day of rain called back to mind, as a song, the verses of Longfellow:

What enchantment the rain!
After the dust and great heat,
in the full and sultry streets,
in the narrow lanes . . .
What enchantment the rain![2]

Testimony C: The Cherries

I am nine years old. I go down by the usual boulevard as far as the bus stop of the academy. I put my schoolbag on the ground for a moment in order to adjust my tassel, and I see (between one moving car and another), and as if I had never seen them before, the cherry trees in bloom. I remain ecstatic, inundated by an unspeakable happiness, isolated from the nearby noise and hurry, as though separated by a circle of fire. I am profoundly aware of my being and feel an immense gratitude towards those trees. All is well.[3]

Testimony D: Evening in the Steppe

It was approaching evening. We were crossing the southern steppe by car. In the gentle and golden light of dusk we were wrapped round in a sweet smell of grass and hay. In the distance, the nearest mountains of the Caucasus were already beginning to be tinged with blue. I was seeing them for the first time. Contemplating them avidly, breathing in the air and light, I listened to that revelation of nature. For a long time I had been used to seeing nothing more in nature than a dead desert under a veil of beauty, as if it wore a deceptive mask.

Then, suddenly, my spirit was filled with joy and trepidation: "And if it were true?" If it were not desert, nor mask, nor death, but Him, the good and loving Father, if nature were His veil which covers His love. . . .

My spirit trembled with amazement. That which had shone for only an instant, and vanished in the evening of the steppe, was now resonating as a song in my heart. The first day of creation was shining before my eyes.[4]

All the testimonies reported suppose a vital purification, at least at the moment of the experience. Our four witnesses would not have been able to have these vivid experiences if even only one of the three vital levels had been blocked by obstacles or turmoils. However, the profundity is not equal in all the cases.

In *testimony A* the experience is reduced to a simple feeling of admiration, provoked by the color of an object being observed. Through attentive eyes the writer perceived all the richness of the yellow color of an envelope, and admiration gave rise to gratitude and familiarity toward that object.

In *testimony B* admiration descends more deeply into the consciousness. The perceptions of the various senses worked together as an ensemble on that bathed day. It is clear that the breadth of the perception carried with it a greater richness and intensity of feelings, shown in the outburst of joy and the poetic level of the description.

Testimony C supposes a step more advanced than the preceding testimonies, even if the protagonist is a child. The profundity and the spiritual elevation are greater. They are expressions of a spiritual reaction that touches religious feeling and a true fullness of joy ("I remain ecstatic, inundated by an unspeakable happiness"). There is a mysterious aspect, indescribable, mystical, that can only be expressed symbolically ("isolated from the nearby noise and hurry, as though separated by a circle of fire"). One remains within a radical silence, where one experiences the greatest intensity of perception (cf. the varied aspects of interior solitude).

Testimony D is the most profound. The experience touches very intense spiritual-religious levels. The protagonist is a young person, twenty-five years old, who has passed a good deal of time in interior emptiness and unbelief. This experience of his cancels all that in an instant and impresses him in the depths of his being. He has the sense of having a revelation, of listening to the revelation of nature ("the heavens declared the glory of God"), and he clearly perceives the life beyond the mask, beyond the superficial zone, the zone he had been used to seeing. The culminating point of this experience is the spiritual vibration: "suddenly, *my spirit* was filled with joy and trepidation"; the name of the divinity revealed itself to him through God's goodness, God's love, God's glory in creatures. When the experience passes, the effects reveal sure signs of the descent of the "good spirit" into the depths of the man, from which is born a distinct vision of life, one that is positive and is full of hope and luminous possibility: "The first day of creation was shining before my eyes."

The Miracle of an Ordinary Day

Why not discover in our own daily life the thousand treasures that the triple purification can offer? We will find ourselves much closer to a life transformed in prayer, even if we have not arrived at the final stages.

Everyone can encounter their own yellow envelope, wonderful rain, cherries in blossom, and the evening that reveals the immense love of God. When love is lived deeply and continuously as if it were a state of life, then one walks toward the contemplative-active level. For the moment we need to convince ourselves that those indescribable revelations are possible even through an insignificant flower, as happened to St. Ignatius in his last years, or in a little drop of water, as this sentence of Taoist mysticism affirms:

> There are moments in which the glance at a flower or the sound of a drop that falls into a lake describes the reality better than all the words of the gigantic encyclopedia of K'ang Hsi.[5]

In other words, our eyes must open to the miracles of every day.

For that reason, now, instead of observing distinct levels of our being, we will attend to the innumerable miracles that surround us.

> The great miracles are those of every day and of every moment, so habitual and gratuitous that we don't take notice of them. That which surprises us is the exception to the rule, but we forget that the rule itself is all one series of miracles. The daily coming and going of our globe, the revolutions of the celestial bodies, their fixed orbits, the dawn and dusk, the regular succession of the seasons, the bouyant racing of the clouds in the sky, their condensation and precipitation in rain, the stupendous development of a bud or the growth of a plant, the air we breathe, the water we drink, the solid ground we tread upon, and the sheer existence of cities . . . all of these marvels have ceased to provoke admiration.[6]

We need to recover the capacity to be in wonder before a drop of water and the growth of a seed. As A. H. Maslow said, the great error of the modern person is not to recognize the miracle in which one is constantly immersed.

> The search for the exotic, for the rare and not the ordinary, has taken the form of pilgrimages, of travels around the world, to the East and to other countries and regions. Meanwhile we often forget the great lesson of the mystics, of Zen monks . . . and, now, even of psychologists; and [so,] the travel can become an easy evasion from the sacred. To go in search of miracles is, for me, a sign of immense ignorance, because everything is a miracle.[7]

The anxious search for wonders, for ones other than such miracles as the lilies of the field and the birds of the sky, is similar to the feverish search of the musk deer that fell, confused, into the precipice. We need to stop, open our eyes, and look about us. If your interior being is purified, if your habitual state is one of silence and calm, free from poisonous desires and interferences, then you are already seeing the miracle of every day. It does not matter where you are or what you are doing, because "everything is a miracle." Then you will continuously perceive the revelation of the miracle. It is like seeing each day the Lord on a chariot passing before you while scattering from full hands thousands of miracles. If men and women open their eyes and feel dazzled by the spectacle, it is because the very light of God that shines through the darkness of the world has illuminated them.

The final adventure, the most transforming of all, which the follower of ardent aspiration can experience in his or her solitary way, is to finally arrive at the source itself of that Light.

Notes

[1] Ernest Wood, *Concentration: An Approach to Meditation* (Madras, India: Adyar, 1966).

[2] Elizabeth Starr Hill, "Hurray! It's raining!" quoted by Mark Link, *In the Stillness Is the Dancing* (Niles, Illinois: Argus Communications, 1972) 40.

[3] Quoted by Nys-Mazure, "La grace d'attention," *La Vie Spirituelle* 611 (1975) 792–3.

[4] Serge Boulgakov, *La lumiere sans declin,* quoted by Giovanni Barra, *Vangelo vissuto* (Turin, Italy: Gribaudi, 1973) 357.

[5] John Blofeld, *Beyond the Gods* (Buddhist and Taoist Mysticism) (London: George Allen and Unwin Ltd., 1974) 25.

[6] Gaspar M. Koelman, *Sparks* (Pune, India: Papal Seminary) 86.

[7] A. H. Maslow, *The Farther Reaches of Human Nature,* quoted by Link, *In the Stillness Is the Dancing,* 18.

CHAPTER EIGHT

The Appearance of the Center

There where your treasure is
there also will be your heart.
(Matt 6:21)

The triple purification of the human being brings about the understanding of life in a greater or lesser profundity according to the level of purity reached. Little by little as the purification becomes more definitive and radical, new riches are discovered every day, till one reaches the point of seeing one's life as a continuous and surprising miracle. God offers this gratuitously to whoever has the eyes to see it. Such understanding supposes, as we have seen, a certain transformation of life, under the light of an initial reflection of contemplation. Certainly, the more one takes into account the marvels that daily surround one, the closer one will come to religious experience. Whoever has reached a state of life of complete purification will sooner or later be attracted by the source of all the wonders, God, the Wonderful One. From the moment in which one's essential inclination is oriented decisively and definitively toward the center, one can say that that one *is already* a contemplative.

The Center

The final step of the way undertaken by ardent aspiration is, therefore, the discovery of the center. "Center" is a word sufficiently clear to indicate in some way the discovery of transcendent things that cannot be defined; it is also generic

63

enough to summarize the varied metaphors with which the mystics express themselves.

The center is then a highly symbolic reality. Scholars of the history of religions tell us that it is one of the most sacred and ancient archetypes of humanity.[1] Accordingly, the center, as symbolic reality, preferably takes on a religious significance. All traditional religions have left us extensive material on this center. In mystical geographies it appears as the sacred space where, in a mysterious and ineffable way, the human being can meet with God. If the center is a place, it will be represented by a temple or by a place within the temple such as the holy of holies of the Temple in Jerusalem. Sacred heights also contain the center, such as Tabor, Calvary, Mount Meru of Oriental Indian tradition, and Garizim, which literally signifies "umbilical cord of the earth"; all indicate a sacred place where heaven and earth unite. The columns of Hercules, the trees of life, the labyrinths of the *mandala* of Oriental Tantrism, and so many other religious symbols take us through distinct routes toward diverse expressions of the same and unique central Reality.

All the different manifestations of the center presume a dynamic approach to it, a "way toward the center." Since we are dealing with a symbolic reality, this way is often ambivalent and apparently contradictory. So, at times one *climbs* to the center, as in the pilgrimages to the Temple of Jerusalem or in the ascent to the Potala, the Sanctuary of Sanctuaries in the holy city of Lhasa in Tibet. In other cases one *descends* to the center, as in the descent to the caverns of the secret initiations in order to obtain a second birth.[2] Thus the center may also be construed as either outside or inside. The combination of these is well represented, for example, in Kundalini-Yoga, in which there is a continual process of penetration into the diverse "subtle centers of energy": the *chakras,* which awaken Kundalini, the serpent energy that sleeps within the heart of every human being and that, rising from center to center along the spine, eventually arrives at the top of the head. Here it meets *Sahasrara,* the "lotus with the thousand petals." When Kundalini reaches *Sahasrara,* illumination and the fullness of ecstasy begin. "The emergence from the self" has led to union with Reality.[3]

As we shall see, elements of a similar mysterious character are also reflected in this way in the center of profound prayer or of contemplative Christian prayer.

We have proposed the triple vital purification as the "way toward the center," a center reachable through the technique and understanding of the one who meditates deeply. The methods of this purifying process are diverse according to periods and cultures, but all agree in requiring an essential purification. Further on, we will see some methods in contemplative Christian experience.

In the following chapter we will discuss the person of Jesus, the Christian center par excellence. As to the genuine difficulty to be found in the language of the mystics, an examination of the diverse modalities, or expressions, of the center will facilitate an understanding of this final and definitive stage of prayer. At the same time it will be helpful to whoever is already involved in the spiritual journey indicated by ardent aspiration to know that the external "adornment" of the center differs according to individual characteristics and circumstances. But the most important point for the contemplative is to know how to discover precisely his or her own supreme center and to adhere to it always. Few things are as clear and secure in the life of the person of profound prayer as the gradual coming to know that the *center discovered is God* or, at least, something that indissolubly ties the person to God. God is the center of centers, and as Nicholas of Cusa affirms: "The poles of the spheres coincide with the center that is God. He is the circumference and center, is in every place and in no place."[4]

The Center as Light

God is light. Scripture and the tradition of the Fathers have constant allusions to the revelation of God-Light. In the well-known description of Wisdom, one reads that she is a "refulgence of the everlasting light."[5] Let us keep in mind that the symbol of light is applied to *the divine essence itself.*

It is not a matter of representing God enveloped in light, clothed in light, creator of light, though these are also frequent expressions in Scripture. The important thing for us is to see how, already in the Old Testament, light appears in direct relationship to the divine essence. The New Testament also presents light in the same sense. So St. John will say, *"God is light* and in Him there is no darkness."[6] St. James calls God "the Father of light."[7] Later on we will see how Christ himself is light and revelation of God-Light.

From antiquity the contemplative Christian tradition presents the mystical center to us as light-center. One of the principal representatives of an actual school centered on the mysticism of the light is Symeon, the New Theologian. In his writings and those of his biographer we can gather how, according to him, the center of contemplative attraction consists of light, a light in direct relationship with the divine essence:

> God is light, and the contemplation of Him is similar to experiencing a light. When we contemplate Him directly, we discern a light, and this sight fills us with wonder; we do not understand it immediately.[8]

In the beginning, then, one goes toward the light with a certain insecurity and timidity. The center has only begun to appear.

One of the most beautiful passages on the mysticism of light is handed down to us by the same Symeon. It is the story of the neophyte who confides to his spiritual father his timid experience of the center:

> If [the neophyte] knows of someone who can explain to him these things because that someone has first known God, then he goes to visit him and says to him: "I have seen." The other replies: "What have you seen, my son?" "A light, father, very exquisite." "Exquisite? But what was the nature of it?" "Well . . ., to tell you the truth, father, I do not rightly understand. . . . When that light appeared to me . . . the space of the room was lifted up and the world disappeared, or more accurately, it fled from the light and I alone remained in the presence of that light. I would not even be able to say, father, if this body of mine was in its place or if it had gone out of it. . . . I do not know . . ., however, I experienced an inde-

scribable joy that I feel even now and, at the same time, such a love and immense desire as to make me shed most abundant tears, just as you see me shedding them in this very moment." The father then replies to him: "It is He, my son, it is really He." After these words [the neophyte] takes account of what is happening to him and little by little accepts the purification. In the measure in which he is purified, he takes courage until he asks the vision itself: "Is it You, my God?" The reply follows: "Yes, it is I. I am the God who was made man for you. Thus have I transformed you and will continue to transform you, as you see, in God."[9]

Here is another recorded experience of the light:

> I see a light that is not of this world. Seated in my cell I see *inside of me* the Creator of the world. I speak with Him, I love Him, and nourish myself on that Divine image. . . .[10]

In this experience the light is interior and central. But in the description of the experience reported by Niceta, biographer of Symeon, the light instead has the antimony of inside-outside:

> *From above* fell a light as of the dawn . . .; little by little it grew, making the air sparkle more and more. He felt that his whole body was leaving behind things here below. That light continued to sparkle always more intensely above him, similar to the bright midday sun. And he understood that *he himself was in the center of the light*. . . . He saw that the light finally enveloped his body, his heart, everything.[11]

The presence of the light as the center that attracts the contemplative is found also in the writings of St. Teresa of Avila. In her, however, the interior light almost always takes the aspect of a luminous fire. Here is how she recounts for us the initial luminous attraction, which she compares to a little spark:

> This prayer is then a spark of the true love of God, that the Lord begins to light in my soul. But if it is God who lights this spark, this, even if tiny, will enkindle the large fire, until it develops (if not suffocated by our own fault) into that inflamed fire of the greatest love for God.[12]

St. John of the Cross speaks also of the light-fire in his noted example of the wood that burns. He makes us see, besides, how essential is the purification of the person before the light will arise, that light of the center, which is found in the depth itself of the contemplative and which transforms the contemplative into a luminous being. After the description of the wood that burns, he adds:

> In the first place it is possible for us to understand how the light and the loving wisdom that is needed to unite with the spirit in order to transform it is the same that at first purifies it and disposes it, just as the fire which transforms the wood by *incorporating it into itself* is that which was first preparing it for this transformation.[13]

The purification obtained by means of the central light is effectively described by this excerpt:

> Since this flame is from a very great light, in colliding with the spirit it penetrates into its most obscure darkness. The spirit then notices the contrast between its natural and flawed darkness and the supernatural light. Thus it will feel the presence of its darknesses because the divine light shines upon them. The spirits, in fact, do not take account of their own darkness if divine light does not besiege them; once they are routed, the spirit will remain illuminated and transformed in light.[14]

In these pages we cannot attend in detail to the mystical characteristics of the light. For our purpose, which is intended to facilitate the life of profound prayer, it will be enough if the person, desirous of purifying the three fundamental levels, remains totally open and attentive to the center of attraction that is manifesting itself. It is possible that that center, for some, appears, in one way or another, as a luminous center. Their contemplative dynamism will consist in opening a way toward the light. God-Light will reveal itself to them little by little, in the beginning stages as a luminous point. But through constant adherence the little spark will transform itself into a large flame. As St. Teresa says, that flame "will grow impetuously" and will "go beyond itself." In its dynamism it will transform everything in the reflection of the eternal light.

The Center as Darkness

We have already said that a paradox of the contemplative center is of manifesting itself in different persons or different moments in apparently contradictory aspects. Thus the reawakening of the center can manifest itself not only in the form of light but also of darkness. Total darkness, mysterious, incomprehensible; yet darkness that attracts. What human explanation can be found when one allows oneself to be seduced by something that is only obscurity, darkness, nothingness?

Scripture tells us that God manifests the divinity as light and yet also as darkness, for in God all antimonies are resolved. The cloud that guided the Israelites in the desert "was dark"[15] and light together.[16] The Bible speaks to us many times of the presence of God in the obscurity of the cloud and of the night. A text full of centrality is one that presents the word of God flung in the middle of the night.[17] Then there is the little verse of Psalm 18 in which it seems God chooses as a tent "a circle of darkness."[18] But the principal text on which the "mysticism of darkness" is based and which parallels that of the light is the story of the theophany of the Exodus, in which God announces to Moses that the One Who Is will be present to him "in a dense cloud"; Moses will approach it, penetrating into its center.[19]

These darknesses symbolize the transcendence and the impenetrability of the divine essence. There is a close relationship here with the very essence of God, even if the language is not as direct as in the case of the light.

Clement of Alexandria and Origen speak to us of this obscurity; but they are theologians more than they are experts on the attraction of the center. St. Gregory of Nyssa, in his last writings, hands down to us the originality and authenticity of his lived experience of the darkness. The darkness progressively attracts the contemplative because God is within it:

> So, disregarding all that which appears—not only that which the senses perceive but also that which the intelligence believes it sees—[the contemplative] proceeds always more toward

the interior until, thanks to the activity of the spirit, it penetrates into the invisible and incomprehensible . . . and it is there that he sees God.[20]

St. Gregory also speaks of the paradoxes of the center:

Here the *seeing* consists in *not seeing*. Therefore the sublime John who penetrated into this *luminous darkness* says that no one has ever seen God, wanting to say that the divine essence is inaccessible not only to the human being but to every intelligent creature.[21]

In the *Commentary on the Canticle of Canticles* St. Gregory of Nyssa describes the beauty of the mysticism of the darkness, the inside/outside, in this poetic form:

Enveloped in the divine night, the soul looks for Him who is hidden in the darkness. It possesses the love of Him whom it desires. However, it escapes the captivity of its thoughts.[22] The soul is wrapped in the divine night, in which the Bridegroom *becomes present . . .* but *he does not show himself to her [the soul].*[23] If you accept me, says God, and you cause me to dwell inside of you, then you will have for recompense the dew that falls on my head and the drops of the night that bathe the curls of my hair.[24]

Here is one of the clearest and most practical expressions on the essence of the gradual attraction of the darkness and where it leads:

Our initial withdrawal from confused and erroneous ideas of God is a passage from darkness to light. Then follows a gradual awareness of hidden things, beyond sensible phenomena, of an invisible world. This awareness is similar to the cloud that covers all appearances, and, little by little, leads and habituates the soul to gaze on that which is hidden there. The soul goes forward and penetrates ever more deeply . . . and when it has released from its shoulders as much as human nature can achieve, then it enters into the secret room of divine awareness and is found completely enveloped by the obscurity of God.[25]

We have seen how St. Gregory calls "the cloud" the darkness of the contemplative. Another phrase familiar to the mysticism of darkness and used by Pseudo-Dionysius is "the Cloud of the incomprehensible": "Then, free from things and from the faculties themselves of contemplation, [the contemplative] enters into the truly mystical cloud of the incomprehensible."[26]

But the author who describes this cloud with greater precision is the humble anonymous author of the fourteenth century, whose well-known book is entitled precisely *The Cloud of Unknowing*. This little book, without evading the depth and difficulty of its theme, has dealt with it with a certain light-heartedness. Above all, it is pervaded by an optimism that removes from the darkness whatever might strike one with exaggerated fear or give the darkness a tragic aspect:

> Now you will say to me: "How will I be able to think of God, just as He is?" To which I can only reply: "I do not know." However, with this question you have taken me inside the darkness itself, and into the cloud of unknowing in which I desire that you enter. . . .
>
> Thought cannot understand God, so I prefer to leave aside what I know and choose to love that which I am not able to know. Even if we are not able to know Him, we can however love Him. He can be touched and embraced by love, never by thought. We do well, naturally, to think of God, of His goodness, for the benefits that such meditation obtains for us. But in authentic contemplative work, we need to leave all this thought aside and cover it with the *cloud of forgetting*.
>
> Therefore, gradually direct your desire of love and adoration until happily and resolutely you penetrate always more and more forward; try even to go through the darkness that covers you. Yes, you strike the cloud of unknowing with the dart of your desire of love, and you must not retreat no matter what happens.[27]

One finds all the terminology of the mysticism of darkness in the *Dark Night* of St. John of the Cross, where the purgative and sorrowful aspect of the darkness stands out in particular:

> Such darkness needs to last for the time necessary in order to annihilate the intellect's habitual way of understanding, which was a long time in use, and to put in its place the illumination of divine light. And so, although the power of

understanding used until this moment by the intellect is natural, it follows that the darkness here suffered is profound, horrible, and very painful, since being perceived in the deep substance of the spirit this darkness seems to be substantial darkness.[28]

This then, briefly said, is the second aspect of the mystical center. Whoever feels attracted to contemplate that dark center will always need to make an effort to be more persuaded or convinced by it, will always need to look at it and more often feel it as a dark pole of attraction. Do not be discouraged, do not ever get weary, and above all do not ever descend to the level of analysis and logical thought. As whoever endeavors to fix their gaze beyond the mist, or better, as a blind person tries to overcome the darkness by obstinately riveting their desire in the darkness without end, so the contemplative needs to fix their loving desire on the dark call that attracts them. Contemplatives do not need to think, or meditate, or reflect, or analyze, but only to love the mysterious and attractive darkness, because when the triple purification will have convinced them of the existence of the ineffable center, that and only that will be the way and the one thing necessary for going further.

Notes

[1] Cf. the profound study of Mircea Eliade on the symbolism of the center, in *Images and Symbols* (New York: Search Books, 1969).

[2] Cf. R. Guenon, *Symboles fondamentaux de la Science Sacree* (Gallimard, 1962) 210–17.

[3] Cf. Arthur Avalon, *Il potere del serpente* (Rome: Mediterranee, 1974). The polarity of the inside-outside of the center appears in this most ancient text of Kundalini Yoga, in which is described the heart (the inside) of the lotus with the thousand petals in which all beings (the outside) share. Reminiscent of Old Testament Wisdom literature is this beautiful description: *"In the inside* there is Nirvana-Kala, the excellent above all excellents. It is subtle as the thousandth part of the point of a hair and has the form of a crescent moon. It is the everlasting Bhagavati, the Devata that *pervades all beings.* It grants divine wisdom and is luminous as the light of all the suns taken together." Op. cit., 341.

[4] Quoted by J. Chevalier and A. Gheerbrant, *Dictionnaire des Symboles* (Paris: Seghers, 1973) 1:299.

[5] Wis 7:26, 29, 30.

[6] John 1:5.

[7] Jas 1:17. The plural Greek, equivalent to "Father of lights," has a strong sense in this context.

[8] *Symeon the New Theologian: The Discourses,* trans. C. J. de Catanzaro (New York: Paulist Press) 192.

[9] Ibid.

[10] *Divinorum amorum liber,* hymn 123, p. 120, 526 c–d.

[11] Niceta Stethatos, *Vie de Symeon le Nouveau Theologien,* n. 69, pp. 94–5, cited by J. Lemaitre in *Dictionnaire de Spiritualite* (Paris: Beauchesne) col. 1853.

[12] Kieran Kavanaugh and Otilio Rodriguez, trans., *Life of Saint Teresa of Avila,* vol. I of *Collected Works of St. Teresa of Avila* (Washington, D.C.: ICS Publications, Institute of Carmelite Studies, 1976) ch. 15; 4, cf. also ch. 19, 4.

[13] *Dark Night,* in *Collected Works of St. John of the Cross,* trans. Kieran Kavanaugh and Otilio Rodriguez (Washington, D.C.: ICS Publications, Institute of Carmelite Studies, 1979) 2, ch. 10, n. 3.

[14] *Living Flame of Love,* in *Collected Works of St. John of the Cross,* first song, 22.

[15] Exod 14:20.

[16] Exod 13:21f.

[17] Wis 18:14f.

[18] Ps 18:12.

[19] Cf. Exod 19:9; 20:21; 24:16.

[20] *Gregory of Nyssa: The Life of Moses,* trans. Abraham J. Malherbe and Everett Ferguson (Paulist Press, 1978).

[21] Ivi.

[22] Ivi, 892–93c.

[23] Ivi, 44, 1001b.

[24] Ivi, 44, 1004a.

[25] Ibid., quoted by G. A. Maloney, *The Breath of the Mystic* (Denville, New Jersey: Dimension Books, 1974) 75.

[26] *Teologia mistica, PG* 1, 1001a.

[27] *The Cloud of Unknowing,* 6:1–4.

[28] *Dark Night,* bk. 2, ch. 9:3.

CHAPTER NINE

Christ as Center

Behold, I am at the
door and knock.
(Ap 3:20)

Christ is the most characteristic center of Christian prayer and contemplation. We have already said how the various aspects of the center lead to the essence of God, and Christ is the revelation of God the Father. Now we will see how the pole of attraction that rises in the depths of the person of profound prayer is not so much a center of light or darkness but rather the person of Christ. Christ, mediator with the Father, participates in some manner in all the characteristics of the various centers of contemplative attraction: he himself is light, darkness, and the unique way toward "the center of centers."

The Mysterious Christ of the Center

In retreat settings and in prayer groups one typically speaks and meditates on Jesus Christ, but the words and reflections often remain in the superficial zone, the farthest away from the center.[1] The same thing may be said of so many movements in vogue (the Jesus revolution, Jesus Christ Superstar) and of certain popular books and works of Christology that present a partial and often superficial aspect of the Christ-center of contemplative experience.

Persons who try daily to encounter Christ with a sincere biblical prayer, with imaginative contemplation or reflective meditation, or through simple dialogue with him would certainly be perplexed if one said to them that the Christ that they imagine, feel, and see is not that true, deep Christ of the contemplative center.²

A parable will clarify this point. Zen monks possess a good repertoire of stories to show us the realities that go beyond concepts and representations. One of these parables presents us with a young widower who lived with his only child, a boy five years old. One day, returning from work, he saw with terror that fire had destroyed his home. Beside himself with desperation, he looked for and called his son. But in vain. When the flames had spent themselves, the charred remains of a child appeared. The father, weeping, collected the ashes and put them in a jewel box in order to preserve them and carry them with him always. That jewel box was his most cherished object, the center of his attention. Fortunately, those ashes were not of his son, who had not been consumed by the fire but had been carried off by bandits. Long afterward the child succeeded in freeing himself and headed for his father's home. He arrived toward midnight. The father was praying, with the box of ashes in his arms. He heard the knocking at the door. "Who is it?" said the father. "It is I, your son; please open the door." "You are lying; my son died many years ago," replied the father. The son continued to knock, but the father, clinging to his ashes, did not open. So he lost his true and only son forever.

Such is the parable. It clearly suggests to Christians that we can often cling obstinately to an idea, a sentiment, or a superficial image of Christ, mistaking it for the true and only reality. Then, as with that father, we could lose forever our true center of attraction.

"Behold, I am at the door and knock. If someone hears my voice and opens the door to me, I will come to him, I will eat with him and he with me" (Ap 3:20).

Who, then, is the Christ of the center? St. Paul, who knew him, describes him in this way:

He is the image of the invisible God,
begotten before any creature;
since by means of him
all things have been created,
things of the heavens and those of the earth,

those visible and those invisible:
Thrones, Dominations,
Principalities and Powers.
All things have been created
by means of him and because of him.
He is the first of all things
and all things exist in him (Col 1:15-17).

Without a doubt these words originate from an experience of the Christ-center. Only thus are understood the power and mysterious grandeur of the words of Paul, a man who one day, on the road to Damascus, had asked the same mysterious Christ, "Who are you?"

Matured by a mysterious and ineffable experience, all who have found the Christ of the center express themselves with similar words.

> This incomprehensible light illumines the mind of the spirit which has entered into itself, because it is the *Eternal Wisdom* that takes form in the soul. Thus the person is transformed from clarity to clarity, that is from a created clarity to one un-created, by means of His eternal image which is the wisdom of the Father.[3]

William of Saint-Thierry describes in a Scholastic style the difference between a superficial Christian experience and one of the center. Without neglecting the usefulness of a reflection on the different aspects of the person of Christ, he gives a glimpse of "a knowledge of Christ that is not according to the flesh":

> One can propose to the beginner, with many other images for meditation, the humanity of the Savior, his birth, his passion and resurrection. . . . The Lord presents himself to us as a mediator; and so, to direct our thought toward him in order to consider Him God under human form is not in fact to depart from the truth. . . . However, as a consequence, faith is transformed into a loving feeling (= knowledge of love), in a delicate embrace of Jesus Christ. Then one begins to see Him no more according to the flesh, even if one still is not able to understand Him completely as God.[4]

St. John of the Cross speaks of the Christ of the center, locating him at the farthest point of a cave: "Therefore we will go away toward the high caverns in the rock that are well hidden and we will enter there."[5]

Then he adds:

> However numerous are the mysteries and wonders the holy doctors have discovered and the holy souls have tested in this state of life, all the more remains for them to say and to understand. So there is still more to fathom in Christ, because He is as a mine with infinite hidden treasures: however deep one goes, one never reaches the bottom. Accordingly, St. Paul said: "In Christ are hidden all treasures and wisdom."[6]

Here lies the "unfathomable richness of the heart of Christ," to be discovered and tasted only in one's true center. Outside of that center all will be, more or less, the "thought of Christ," according to its nearness to the superficial zone. But the Christ of unfathomable richness, the mysterious One, he whom, so many times, we have called "heart of Christ," is precisely the Christ of the center.

William Johnston speaks of the fusion of the two centers: that of the contemplative, descended into the depth of his or her own heart, and that of the mysterious Christ, discovered in the depth:

> The living and risen Christ of Paul, the one who lives always in the human person, is the unknowable Christ, co-extensive with the universe and hidden in the deepest recesses of the human heart. In the depths of the heart of Paul there is not Paul but Christ; Paul does not live but Christ lives in Him; it is not Paul who cries out: "Abba, Father" but the spirit of Christ that is within him. For Paul, to live is Christ, to die is Christ and it is all the same thing. If that is true for Paul, it is true also for anyone who believes; in the depth of the believer there is not oneself but Christ.[7]

Christ in the Heart of the Yogi

These words of William Johnston remind us of the profound experience of the Christ of the center, obtained thanks to the *japam* (a technique of classical Yoga that many compare to the "Jesus prayer") practiced by the yogi Amaldas Brahmachari:

78

One day I began to meditate together with an American woman, my teacher of Yoga. I indicated a rock to her that she could sit on, while I went to another one. I sat in the position of the padmasana and began to repeat the name of Jesus. Looking around, I was able to see mountains, valleys, cities, and cows pasturing nearby. While I observed that most beautiful panorama, I praised God for having created all those things and for manifesting Himself in them.

After a certain time, my eyes and my mouth closed, but the invocation continued in my heart and in rhythm with my breathing. Every time I repeated the holy name of Jesus, I realized that I was coming ever closer to Him.

I began to feel a force that was pushing me toward Christ and bringing me to union with Him. I call this force that had been revealed to me, the Spirit of Christ, given to me by the Father. . . .

My innermost awareness began to make me understand that my body was united to that of Christ and my blood to the blood of Christ.

Then, I experienced the sensation of becoming ever larger, as if the whole universe was transformed in my body and all creation itself was inside me. Gradually I began to perceive that that was not my body but the universal body of Christ Jesus, of the Cosmic Christ.

Thereafter I sensed a succession of changes within me, perceiving that a great happiness existed in the life *beyond myself* and that the heavenly Father was much *more in me* than I myself.

In that moment it seemed to me that I was sharing in the divine life. I could not distinguish my body from that of the Cosmic Christ; I seemed to be part of the universal body in which all of humanity is inserted. I, Christ, and the Father were there, and this universal human person was full of the Holy Spirit.[8]

Look at This Heart

Speaking of the center, we have always said that the proper action of contemplatives, faithful to their discovery, is simply to gaze at that which attracts them in the center of their being. Not to think but to look at; not to discuss, not even to try to understand or to analyze but to look at the attracting center, allowing oneself to be always more conquered by that attraction. This is true also for the mysterious Christ of the center: when he invites one to know him in a total and transforming way, he simply says, "Look at this heart," that is, "Look at the center of centers." This, then, is the paradox, one ever old and ever new, of the unfathomable richness of Christ: the one who knows how to look at it must do so; whoever has ears to hear should listen. But it is necessary to know how to look in the darkness and how to listen to the most tenuous summons. Everything else just keeps one in the superficial zones. Because of this an ancient abbot of the desert said to his disciples; "The knowledge of Christ does not have need of a spirit capable of dialectic but a spirit that knows how to look, for even the impure can acquire dialectic, while contemplation resides solely in the pure."[9]

The Game of Little Baruch

In a page of his *Diary,* Julien Green tells of little Baruch, son of a rabbi, who was playing hide-and-seek with his friend. The little boy stayed for a good deal of time in his hiding place. When finally he decided to go out in the open, he realized that his playmate was no longer there. Then Baruch burst into tears and ran in search of his father to tell him, "I hide and no one wants to find me." On hearing these words, the old rabbi could not stop the boy's tears and exclaimed, "God does not speak differently: 'I am hiding and no one wishes to find me.'"

This is the paradox. He who is calling at the door and says, "Look at this heart," is, in a certain way, hidden, and speaks from that hiding place. It is necessary to accept the rules of the game of little Baruch if we wish to discover who calls us. If someone opens to him and listens to him only in a superficial way, then that one will discover only a superficial Christ. But whoever has been purified in the three levels breaks the crust of the superficial, listens to the mysterious call of the center, accepts the rules of little Baruch, and begins the great search. There is nothing to do but to let oneself always be grasped more by the "game" of searching. Then Christ, who lives by faith in our hearts, will illuminate us with his unique and mysterious light.

Notes

[1] See drawing on page 57.

[2] Naturally, I do not wish to say that the daily meeting with Jesus, in any sincere prayer, is false or unbecoming. But according to all that has been said regarding the "center of the human person" (ch. 8), the meeting with Christ in prayer will need to be evaluated in the light of our distance from or nearness to that center.

[3] Ruysbroeck, *Reign of Lovers*, c. 39. Cf. *Collationes Brugenses*, t. 26, pages 441ff.

[4] *Epistula ad Fratres*, bk. 1, c. 14, n. 43: *PL* 184, 336a–b.

[5] *Spiritual Canticle*, strophe 37, in *Collected Works of St. John of the Cross*, trans. Kieran Kavanaugh and Otilio Rodriguez (Washington, D.C.: ICS Publications, Institute of Carmelite Studies, 1979).

[6] Ivi, Red B.

[7] William Johnston, *Christian Zen*, c. 6.

[8] Amaldas Brahmachari, *Yoga, esercizi, preghiere, unione* (Bologna: EMI, 1977) 45–6.

[9] Evagrius Ponticus, *Cen.* 4, 90 (Frankenburg) 317.

CHAPTER TEN

How to Look at the Center

Blessed are those who, on his return, the master will find still awake.

(Luke 12:37)

Knowing How to Look

The center being found, the essential task of deep prayer consists entirely in knowing how to look at it. Upon this depends the steady growth and the innumerable benefits of contemplation.

Nicholas Caballero expresses the advantages of knowing how to look:

> When one looks at one thing without entangling something else with it, it appears in its true light. One excludes nothing of what one is looking at because one does not distort it with one's own ideas, opinions, experiences, or prejudices. Such subjective factors not only distort things of the world in which we live; they also distort the reality of God.[1]

For whoever is purified in their three levels of life, be it even in an elementary way, the "factor of distortion" of which Caballero speaks will be considerably reduced. Thus the center will begin to show forth its riches. Nevertheless, it is necessary to know concretely and exactly *how* to look. How does one do it, in practice, in order not to become bewildered and uselessly waste time? Does a technique for learning to look exist?

Concentration

Yoga, especially Raja Yoga, offers us a precious help on this subject through its use of the technique of *dharana,* which means "concentration," that is, *fixing the mind on one object only.* The masters of Yoga begin by teaching the disciples concentration on simple and concrete objects: a particle of crystal, a point on the wall, a tiny flower. A little at a time they raise the spiritual quality of the object, eventually passing on to the nature of virtue, to the ideals of the disciple, and finally to God, synthesized in a supreme Name. This final stage, the most important and definitive of Raja Yoga, is equivalent to the essential concentration spoken of in this book: *looking at the center.*

Some masters, especially Western, insist from the beginning on the technique of *knowing how to look,* without concerning themselves much about whether the disciple is already opened to the supreme attraction of the center. Such an approach renders concentration more difficult for the disciple insofar as the disciple is not yet purified in the three vital levels. An infinity of thoughts, feelings, and tensions will intervene between the disciple and the object on which he or she is concentrated. Therefore a preferable method is one that gives priority to the triple purification and to the guidance of the person through his or her ardent aspiration toward God. Such a method can be adapted from the very ancient way of Raja Yoga, which begins by requiring the practice of the purifying disciplines of *yama* and *niyama.* As a consequence of practicing these two disciplines, the moment will arrive when one passes to the practice of *dharana.* I believe that the strange and intense sufferings that appear with frequency in the life of mystics are often caused by this critical phase: when, on the one hand, the pray-er wishes to gaze intensely at the center and on the other, feels the continual interference of their own being, not yet entirely purified.

Samyama

The complete exercise of the *continuous gaze* toward the center of Yoga is called *samyama* (from *yama,* control, and *sam,* complete). The *samyama* is practiced, in the beginning, with the technique of *dharana,* or concentration. When the mind, thanks to the continual practice of looking fixedly, can apply itself to the concentration of an object without interference or weariness, then one says that they are practicing *dhyana,* that is, a prolonged concentration. The *dhyana* practice leads to *samadhi,* that is, the state of perfect fusion between the subject contemplating and the object contemplated.

The most important and elementary point of the *samyama* is, then, the continued and simple application of the mind to the center, that is, the practice of *dharana* on the center.

Exercise 1: Dharana

1. Begin saying to yourself that you are going to concentrate and that you have decided that you want to control your mind. Involve yourself as much as possible in the action that God is unfolding in you: to expose yourself and make yourself more and more known in the center of your being. "Behold, I am at the door and knock." Believe that you will succeed in opening the door to God, as so many others have succeeded in doing.

2. Choose a comfortable and relaxed position, helping yourself with some of the relaxation exercises advised in the preceding chapters.

3. Raise your prayer to Christ, your first *guru* (master), and tell him that he is to direct the steps of your mind and fix it solely on your center, completely removing everything else.

4. Then, fix your mental gaze on your Supreme Center. Remember: the center can present itself localized in your heart, in your mind, or even outside of you—for example, in a very elevated place such as "the Father who is in heaven." It is important that you look at it *where you find it* and that you gaze at it with attention, in great silence, that you do nothing else.

5. At the beginning (during the first weeks or first months) the *dharana,* or concentration, requires considerable effort. It is necessary not to forget, though that effort does not at all mean tension. The effort consists in an infinite patience in returning to fix the gaze on the center every time the mind is distracted. For this purpose it can be useful to avail oneself of a support, such as a supreme name of God

(for example, "God," or "Love," or "Jesus"). The more brief and simple the support, the more will it facilitate concentration. The name is only a help for the beginner; one should tend toward having the *experience of the center* more than of the name of the center. Others, who are perhaps less religious, will find a useful support in the awareness of the rhythm of the breath.

6. Within the first months of an assiduous and intense application of the exercise one comes to acquire, even if amidst difficulties, a remarkable awareness of the more subtle and inadvertent ways with which the mind functions, of the games and subterfuges it puts into play in order not to be controlled. Little by little, however, the mind itself will discover the marvels of *dharana*, of the silent and attentive gaze: then will be opened to it a whole unexplored and truly attractive world.

7. The time of dedication to the *dharana* varies according to individuals and the mental maturity of each person. It is important therefore not to weary or do violence to the mind. When a sixth sense cautions that it is not appropriate to continue the exercise (we are not speaking here of distraction, but of incapacity, of momentary weariness), it is well to set it aside for awhile.

A standard time to begin with can be twenty minutes a day. Serious and assiduous practice will naturally tend to prolong the exercise. Each person will take into account what he or she can do and then do that, even with joy.

Exercise 2: Active Concentration

Some yogis also advise concrete exercises of meditation, or active concentration, that can be practiced not only during the *dharana* but throughout the day.

Active concentration consists in pronouncing as frequently as possible the name of the center as a spontaneous and habitual reaction during the day—passing from one activity to another, waiting for the bus, walking, and so on.

That name has to be one of the names for light when one needs discernment, strength, courage, comfort, and love in the face of suffering and sorrow. In the beginning the name should be pronounced mentally; eventually it will be enough to live the experience in and with that name, without pronouncing it even mentally.

The privileged moment of union with the center is the time immediately before sleep. What happens in that moment penetrates into the subconscious and has an influence on the person. St. Ignatius of Loyola had a profound intuition about the function of these human mechanisms; a proof is given in his famous additional directives in the *Spiritual Exercises.* Speaking of the control of the emotions, he offers his first addition precisely as a suggestion to use before sleeping.[2] All that one need do, then, is to repeat that name or to connect oneself to the experience one has of the name as soon as one notices the proximity of sleep.

The Three Stages of Assimilation of *Dharana*

The sanctification of the subconscious is a theme little treated by our Christian theologians or masters of the spirit,[3] but it is familiar terrain for the traditional schools of Yoga. Putting it concisely, we could say that the recommended exercises aim at the energy of the center continuously sanctifying first the conscious level; then, when the energy of the center is freed by concentration, it will pass on to sanctifying the subconscious. When a person experiences this double and continuous sanctification, the energy of the center will open them to the level of the superconscious and thus to *samadhi,* or illumination.

What we have said up to now is only intended to be an orientation. I repeat once again: the principal work in the movement toward the center comes down to the individual's continuous practice. The experience of concentration is a fact as personal and untransferable as individuality itself. More strongly: it is the very essence of the individual that is changed in a continuous awareness and gaze toward the supreme attraction. Only you can discover, by yourself, what is the mysterious and infinite adventure of looking toward the center. The rules set forth are only the support for an elementary initiation. Here we simply repeat the eternal truth called to mind by the poet Machado: "The journey is made by walking."

Notes

1   *Il cammino della liberta,* 3 (Valencia: Edicep, 1976) 138.

2   Ignatius of Loyola, *Spiritual Exercise and Selected Works,* ed. George Ganss (New York: Paulist Press, 1991) 142.

3   Karl Rahner has an interesting theological study of this theme in *La fede in mezzo al mondo* (ed. Paoline, 1981).

CHAPTER ELEVEN

The Signs

A good tree cannot
produce evil fruit.
(Matt 7:18)

The final stage of our course on the distinct aspects of profound prayer is to fix our attention on some signs that appear in the life of the contemplative.

"Every tree is known by its fruits," says the Lord (Luke 6:44). St. Paul lists the fruits in order to know who belongs to one side or the other, who has truly discovered the center, and who still nourishes "desires contrary to the Spirit" (Gal 5:16-26). Observe, however, that the signs, considered separately, are not something infallible. It is their presence taken together that gives the best guarantee for knowing to what extent a person is a contemplative who has discovered the center.

I would like, moreover, to underline a particular aspect: the "fruits of the Spirit," as St. Paul calls them, *are* fruits. They are therefore not something to be sought after or to be constructed through our own volition and determination. The true fruit is one that is discovered; it is an effect, or outcome, and not a cause. Thus in the physical order a tree and the person who cultivates it and makes it grow exist before the fruit does. It would be an error, accordingly, if one insisted on desiring the fruit-signs directly and prematurely, because they would then not have the genuine reality that comes only from the trunk and the roots.

Let us consider now the signs that appear in the true contemplative.

1. Joy

Joy is born spontaneously from the depths of the heart of one who can contemplate the lilies of the field in all their splendor. Recall what we have said about the luminosity and optimism that surrounds the life of the one who has purified the three levels of their being. If then God has begun to wield the divine and exquisite attraction from the depth and from the center, that person's life will erupt in ever more genuine and silent happiness.

> It seems to me, without any doubt, that contemplation is the joyous hymn of the love of God that invades the human mind with the gentleness of an angelic praise. It is a heavenly joy existing on earth. Therefore says the psalmist: "Blessed the one who knows exultation," the exultation of the contemplation of God.[1]

These words sum up one of the most repeated themes of the masters of meditation and contemplative prayer of every age and every religion: by its nature, contemplative prayer ends with joy. Paramahansa Yogananda describes thus the beginning of contemplative joy:

> Given that your soul is a reflection of the Spirit, which is eternally happy, your soul substantially enjoys the same happiness. If you keep the eyes of your concentration closed you will not be able to see the sun of happiness that shines on your breast. However, in as much as you narrow the eyes of your attention [as it were, mentally squinting in order to see somewhat], the rays of happiness will stretch continuously to go beyond the closed threshold of your mind. Open the windows of the stillness and you will see erupt suddenly in your deepest self the sun of joy![2]

Enomiya Lassalle, enumerating the fruits produced by a "Zen Christian path," that is, by the application of Eastern techniques to contemplative Christian prayer, expresses it thus: "The fifth [fruit] is an interior joy and harmony that renders the person continuously satisfied and happy, capable of taking pleasure with all their being in every good and beautiful thing."[3]

The joy of the contemplative, according to the stages that he or she is going through, can have multiple nuances in quality and intensity, but this joy is always an incontestable fact, since one is approaching the very font of joy. "Your heart will rejoice and no one can take from you your joy," says Jesus to the disciples, referring to the interior transformation that the coming of the Holy Spirit will work in them (John 16:22).

2. Peace

The interior peace and serenity of the contemplative is another sign described by the various schools of prayer.

It is a peace that originates from a progressive liberation. The searcher has passed through a process of liberation that has, little by little, freed him or her from attractions and revulsions originating from an erroneous vision of reality. When beginning to look at reality in all its splendor, the person understands by experience the stupidity of clinging to one's own soul egoistically, as if the human soul were *the* center, and not rather a way toward or a reflection of that center. The serenity, the visible calm of holy contemplatives even in sorrowful situations, is a proof of the existence of this sign. The famous "indifference" before creatures suggested by St. Ignatius of Loyola in the *Beginning and Foundation* of his *Exercises*[4] greatly resembles this profound contemplative peace, especially if it is considered as the spontaneous and gentle fruit of a fundamental attitude of the person: to seek above all the Creator.

In her last years, St. Teresa of Avila looked at the complications and noises of this life as pale and fleeting images of a dream:

> Finding myself outside the world, in a little and holy company, I look at things as from above and am little bothered by what they say or know about me. The Lord makes me see things as in a dream; I seem to be almost always dreaming about how much I see. I experience neither contentment nor suffering, however great. If an incident strikes me, the reaction passes so quickly that I am surprised at myself and it seems to me that I have dreamt it. Truthfully, if I wanted to

> rejoice in it or be sad in it, it is not in my power, as could happen to anyone who wished to rejoice or be saddened by something that was dreamed. This happens to me because the Lord has reawakened my soul, detaching it from all that which, when I was not being mortified and dead to the world, held me enthralled; and His Majesty does not wish me to return there.[5]

This passage is taken from the last chapter of Teresa's autobiography and therefore corresponds to a sign of the most mature and elevated stage of her contemplative journey.

Nevertheless, the peace of which we speak does not always assume such radical characteristics. All will depend on the path of the person who meditates in depth. At the beginning, however, one will marvel at the acquired control of oneself in facing daily life. The occasions that used to be irritating no longer are so; they lose importance and disappear, giving place to peace and serenity. Enomiya Lassalle, cited above, tells us in this regard, "The third fruit is the custody of interior peace and the dominion of oneself amidst all the vexations of daily life."[6]

3. Cosmic Awareness

Among the signs that appear in the life of the active contemplative, the least considered one is the progressive expansion of awareness. Modern studies on Eastern meditation, or so-called natural illumination, bring out this important aspect, which undoubtedly enters into Christian contemplation also.

When the awareness of the contemplative discovers, in whatever way, its "center of centers," there is produced in it something like an expansion of the interior horizon, with varying degrees and aspects according to its intensity and perdurance. We give here an example of intellectual expansion that appeared suddenly and with great intensity in the life of St. Ignatius of Loyola. He never forgot the day when he sat down, tired, near the river Cardoner. His mind was already used to contemplation; in fact, he was already an expert in prayer. All of a sudden, yet quietly, his mind was immersed in the thought of God.

While he was seated there [he dictates to Fr. Gonzalvez de la Camera in his autobiography], the eyes of his intellect were opened. It was not a vision, but he knew and understood many principles of the interior life and many divine and human things with such light that all appeared to him as if new. It is not possible to refer with clarity to the numerous particular truths that he then understood. One can only say that he received a great light in the intellect. Experiencing the intellect illuminated in such a way was so intense that it seemed to him that he was another man or that his intellect was different than what it was before. So that if he took into account all the things learned and all the graces received from God and put them together, he did not seem to have learned as much through the course of his life, up to 62 years of age, as he had that one single time.[7]

The expansion of consciousness can come gradually:

We live in a planetary epoch in which human beings desire to liberate themselves from nationalistic straits in order to re-build the earth in a universal spirit. Observing the place occupied by our tiny planet in the immense complexity of the universe, they aspire to act in a cosmic way. If the meditation which we have set forth in this work holds an appeal for the contemporary person, this is in a certain sense because of its cosmic implications. Meditation in fact entails an expansion of consciousness, a loss of the "self," a threshold to altered states of consciousness, an impulse toward a dimension that passes beyond space and time so that not only the human spirit, but the psyche and body are in some way made cosmic.[8]

The cosmic consciousness of the authentic contemplative is a clear response to the recurring objection about his or her isolation. In fact, the more contemplative one is, the more cosmic are one's vital activities, even in the most apparently insignificant details. The Christian contemplative life, then, is gradually cognizant of participating in the mystical body of Christ, of a Christ who is the "center of the cosmos and of history."[9]

The masters of Raja Yoga teach their disciples the *niyama,* an exercise that helps expand the consciousness of the one who has started profound prayer. It is not a matter of direct pursuit of the expansion of consciousness, since the expansion is, rather, a sign, a consequence of the contemplative life. The masters of Raja Yoga, in fact, wish to help the disciples discover how much already exists in the depths of their being and that is already being revealed as an ordinary condition, thanks to the degree of their contemplation. Besides, cosmic awareness is an altogether realistic attitude that reveals itself suddenly in everything.

> Open your eyes, look around you and observe how the world suffers from the lack of a cosmic awareness. You know that cosmic awareness is not a matter of abstractionisms or of a form of "spiritualism." It is the truth, and truths are facts that can be proved with the physical sciences and modern psychology. This cosmic awareness is an attitude, a way of thinking possible to everyone. It consists in recognizing that if what I desire is a good only for me and not for everyone and everything, in the end it is not even a good for me. If I try to satisfy those desires for myself alone, they then cause suffering. However, if those desires foster something good for everyone under every aspect, they need to be cultivated with enthusiasm, until they are realized. Not one desire exists, no matter how little or insignificant, that does not assume wide-ranging effects. Desires are energies that penetrate walls, go beyond mountains, time and space.[10]

4. Health

One could speak at length of the fruits of physical and psychic health that are manifested in those who apply themselves to profound prayer. Naturally, there are exceptions in which history shows us cases of contemplative life associated with sickness. But I want only to underline the fact that profound prayer puts body and spirit perfectly into harmony. It will be enough to remember what was said regarding the triple purification of the human being. The deeper the contemplative prayer, the more positive will be the influence on the body. So-called psychosomatic medicine, currently so much in vogue, is a proof.

> Recently a marked interest has been noted in meditation as therapy. Western medicine has till now been too unilateral,

widely ignoring the contribution of the mind in the cure of the human body. It is now acknowledged that 80% of modern illness has a psychosomatic origin. Only now with the increased influence of the East and talk about acupuncture, learning the system of vital energies . . . have the spiritual and metaphysical aspects of healing begun to be taken into account. The interest is growing, and it is not hazardous to suppose that meditation will become one of the principal means of the therapy of the future.[11]

5. Familiarity with the Mystery

Whoever is acquainted with the writings of the contemplatives finds the sign of their experience and ease with the world of mysteries. The mystics find it difficult, of course, to express the inexpressible; but they succeed in moving with agility in that world and even to communicate somehow their indescribable experience. The difficulty of communication comes not so much from them as from the common person, who thinks impossible and too elevated the strange and transcendent world of the contemplative life. But it is logical and inevitable that this be so. Some know how to see beyond the lilies of the field, while others see only Solomon and the immediate reflection of his material riches. These are two worlds, two languages that will find mutual comprehension difficult.

> Investigators of the field of consciousness do not have words to express that complex world: perhaps this is the reason for their growing interest in mysticism and mystics themselves. The problem does not have an easy solution, because it is impossible to speak adequately of altered or expanded states of consciousness with words taken from normal vocabulary. It would be like being at the same time a citizen of two different worlds and wanting to put them in contact with each other. For this reason the mystics, in order to express themselves, resort ordinarily to symbolism or to silence.[12]

It is no wonder, then, that the mystics have often been considered by their contemporaries to be extravagant dreamers or fools. In fact, this is how some rationalists interpret the comparisons of St. Teresa of Avila or the intricate metaphors of the poems of St. John of the Cross, because they are inclined to think that all these mystics' writings are only celestial music. And in a sense they are right. It *is* a matter of a music, of a mysterious language detected only by contemplatives. It is as if only they possessed the key for harmonizing with the mystery, with what is beyond the perceptible sound, beyond the material significance of things and events. "Whoever has ears to hear, hear," the Lord frequently said after his parables.

The Three Signs of St. John of the Cross

St. John of the Cross in two passages, by now classics of his writings, offers us three key signs to recognize contemplatives: three "traffic lights" that open the way to contemplative prayer and discourage the continuance of any prayer of a discursive type. He very aptly points out that the three signs manifest themselves simultaneously and that just one of them, taken in isolation, loses the value of a contemplative sign.[13]

I can do nothing more in prayer. One frequently hears people who have for years practiced discursive prayer express themselves in this way: "I believe I am not doing anything in prayer" or "I am losing time in prayer." In reality, for the contemplative "doing nothing" means something different; it indicates the passivity of the reason and the diminishing need of words. The person becomes more truly contemplative precisely when he or she vaguely understands that there is a need to pray in a different way and to do everything possible to learn to behave more passively. Resorting to the world of paradoxes, so familiar in this type of prayer, we would say that it is a matter of "acting passively." Therefore, the lighting of this pilot light that manifests itself as boredom, powerlessness, and repugnance of discursive prayer is not a temptation but the first traffic light that can open the way to go beyond the simply factual lilies of the field.

Nothing attracts me. St. John of the Cross describes the second stop-and-go light, one similar to states of general depression about the material world, as "not investing the imagination and the senses in other particular things." St. Ignatius defines it with the word "indifference." Let us remember, however, that it is a sign: it is a detachment and an indifference that is *not so much sought after as discovered,* appearing spontaneously in the contemplative.

The most secure sign. So St. John of the Cross calls his third traffic light. It is the most secure sign because it qualifies and determines in a radical and unique way the contemplative orientation of the other two. Using the terms employed up till now, we could say that the third sign is the discovery of the center as the *one thing necessary,* the discovery, that is, of God-Love, who attracts us in a total and absolute way:

> The third and most secure sign is when the spirit rejoices in being alone, with loving attention to God, without particular considerations and in interior peace, quiet, and repose, without act or exercise of its powers—intellect, memory, will. . . . The spirit is solely attentive and lovingly present, as we have said, without any particular knowledge or understanding.[14]

The clearest and most authentic sign, therefore, that appears in the contemplative is none other than love. Fundamentally, it is the first and second commandment of Jesus, the compendium of the Law and the Prophets. Even more, it is the "beyond the law,"[15] as it is also the "beyond the lilies."

Notes

[1] Richard Rolle, *The Amending of Life,* trans. M. L. del Mastro (Garden City, N.Y.: Image Books, 1981) 85–6.

[2] *Meditazioni metafisiche* (Rome: Astrolabio, 1974) 65.

[3] Enomiya Lassalle, *Zen, un cammino verso la propria identita* (Bilbao: Mensajer, 1975) 147.

[4] Cf. Ignatius of Loyola, *Spiritual Exercises and Selected Works,* ed. George Ganss (New York: Paulist Press, 1991) n. 23.

[5] Kieran Kavanaugh and Otilio Rodriguez, trans., *Life of St. Teresa of Avila,* vol. 2 of the *Collected Works of St. Teresa of Avila* (Washington, D.C.: ICS Publications, Institute of Carmelite Studies, 1976) ch. 40, n. 22.

[6] Lassalle, *Zen,* 147.

7   *Opere complete* (Madrid: BAC, 1963(2)) 104–5.

8   William Johnston, *Silent Music* (London: Collins, 1974) 132.

9   John Paul II, *Redemptor hominis*, 1.

10   C.E.S. RAI, *Lezioni di Raja-yoga* (Rome: Mediterranee, 1975) 2:144–8.

11   Johnston, *Silent Music*, 107.

12   Ivi, 55.

13   *Ascent of Mount Carmel*, in *Collected Works of St. John of the Cross*, trans. Kieran Kavanaugh and Otilio Rodriguez (Washington, D.C.: ICS Publications, Institute of Carmelite Studies, 1979) vol. 2, 13; and vol. 1 *Dark Night*, 9.

14   *Ascent of Mount Carmel*, 13, n. 4.

15   Cf. Gal 5:22-23.

Conclusion

We have seen in these pages some aspects of true prayer, of the active contemplation and deep prayer that transforms and perfects life. In examining the various stages of this gradual transformation of the human being, it was said that it all begins in a search (at first timid and obscure, then clearer and more concrete, according to the individual) that is always immersed in the wonderful outburst of an ardent desire for God. It was necessary to describe a way of purification in a triple ascesis, required so that the initial impulse of search not be exhausted in vain desires and in wandering useless paths like those of the musk deer. We have seen how the triple purification—physico-muscular, emotional, and mental—has the concrete purpose of revealing to the eyes of the contemplative the beauty of daily life, until that life becomes a stupendous and ongoing miracle. The most authentic and definitive stage of the search is, however, the discovery of the contemplative center. That center is the point of attraction that manifests itself according to the culture and personality of the one searching, but always in direct relationship to the personal God. After this, one has no more to do than to gaze at the center and to adhere constantly to that pole of supreme attraction of all one's being. This is—with certain nuances we have hinted at here and there—the best activity, the surest way to arrive at the highest level of spiritual maturity without squandering our energies.

It is easy to conclude from all this how important it is to look for and discover the center of attraction. When a person has not yet found it and has known it only in theory, such a one feels deprived of the strength that gives unity and cohesion to one's life, a strength that elevates one's destiny and transforms it into a constant vision that overcomes the world that surrounds one, overcomes the restriction of a conception of life that is purely earthly, momentary, and myopic. The man or woman, old or young, who is deprived of the divine center of attraction will live with the mind exposed to the continuous influences of the environment. Such persons will not know how to discern the good from the bad. They will lack a purpose and, above all, the guiding force that reveals in them the best ideals and qualities to elevate and integrate in personal unity and originality.

On the contrary, when one comes to discover one's supreme center, the miracle of life will be revealed; the personality will elevate itself more and more; there will remain open before one a wide road; and it will acquire cosmic dimensions, because every center, whatever its form, leads only to God, since God is infinite. Everything depends on the constancy and intensity with which the contemplative gazes at the center of centers. But meanwhile, the way has been discovered; it is enough only to travel it to the end. What is needed most is love, and all the mysteries and greatness of a unique and true love.

It is love that builds the earth and carries forward the impulse of evolution. It is love that reunites the great traditions into a prolific union compatible with the differences. It is love that carries all toward the Omega, the point of convergence, which is also

> The mountains
> the lonely and woody valleys,
> the strange islands
> the silent music.[1]

At the beginning of this book I told the legend of the musk deer, the story of a search that ended badly because it lacked love. I want to end the journey we have taken together by telling another story.

Still today in India people know the songs of Mirabai. This princess of the Middle Ages abandoned the life of the court, moved by an intense desire for God. She felt herself pervaded by the extraordinary power of God's love. Her life was not easy, but the power of love was greater than the obstacles she encountered. The words of the song of Mirabai will close these pages, since they form the best epilogue concerning the way of integration that we have traveled.

> If, bathing oneself every day, one was able to remain in God
> I would want to be a whale in the bottom of the sea.
> If, eating fruit and roots, we were able to understand Him
> I would happily choose the form of a goat.
> If, counting the beads of the rosary, we were able to discover
>   Him
> I would recite my prayers with infinite rosaries.
> If, bowing before statues of stone, we were able to awaken
>   Him
> I would humbly adore a mountain of rock.
> If, drinking milk, one was able to absorb the Lord
> Many lambs and infants would know Him.
> If, leaving one's own wife, one attracted the Lord
> Thousands of men would make themselves eunuchs.
> Mirabai knows that in order to meet God
> *the one indispensable thing is love.*[2]

Notes

[1] William Johnston, *Silent Music* (London: Collins, 1974) 174.
[2] Paramahansa Yogananda, *Autobiography of a Yogi.*

Glossary of Terms

asana. Position.

chakras. Centers of energy that awakens Kundalini.

chakrasana. Position of the wheel.

dharana. Concentration, or fixing the mind on one object only.

dhyana. Prolonged concentration.

guru. Master.

japam. A technique of classical Yoga.

nispanda bhava. Simple awareness of sounds.

nivama. An exercise in Raja Yoga that helps expand the consciousness during profound prayer.

padmasana. Supreme lotus position.

pratyahara. Withdrawal of the senses.

Sahasrara. Lotus with the thousand petals.

samadhi. Illumination; that is, the state of perfect fusion between the subject contemplating and the object contemplated.

samyama. Exercise of the continuous gaze toward the center.

shavasana. Position of the corpse.

sutra. A series of little spiritual verses.

suwari. A position.

vajrasana. Position of the diamond.

yama. Control; a purifying discipline of Raja Yoga.